Diary of a Public School Board Member

Dr. Karen Hiltz

The Apple Report
Copyright © 2020 Dr. Karen Hiltz
ISBN: 978-1-970153-24-8
Library of Congress: 2020918059

No part of this publication may be reproduced or transmitted in any form or by any means, graphic, electronic, photocopy, recording, or by any information storage retrieval system—except for excerpts used for published review—without the written permission of the Author.

Cover image - Victory Store - Davenport, Iowa

La Maison Publishing, Inc.
Vero Beach, Florida
The Hibiscus City
lamaisonpublishing@gmail.com

Testimonials

I can identify with the experiences of Dr. Hiltz and I'm thankful that she has brought these issues to light. We need more people like her to be willing to run for their local School Boards to make a difference for our students.

> Victoria Manning
> Virginia Beach School Board Member
> Virginia Beach, VA

Karen has the ability to dissect a problem quickly and to bring attention to the issues that need to be addressed, which I always appreciated. She served Franklin County in appointed and elected positions and her contributions are missed.

> Bob Camicia
> Former Gills Creek District Supervisor
> Franklin County, VA

Dr. Hiltz has her finger on the pulse of public policy and worked tirelessly as a School Board member to promote sound administrative processes that enhanced student-learning environments. Words describing Dr. Hiltz include professional, caring, knowledgeable, and accountable.

> Lorie M. Smith
> Gills Creek District Supervisor
> Franklin County, VA

Dr. Hiltz and I served on the School Board together. Even though ideologically we are polar opposites, we found common ground and purpose requesting that the board instill documented board governance, consistent HR policies, and measurable goals. I hope this book inspires you to get involved in your local school system.

Penny E. Blue
Franklin County School Board Member
Franklin County, VA

It takes a special kind of person to take on the-good-old-boy's educational establishment, especially in smaller counties far away from the metro centers of the east coast. Tradition, local pride, and history form a strange kaleidoscope through which the public sees their schools. Karen did that and lived to tell about it.

Mark Young
Campaign Committee Member

It was a pleasure to serve on Karen's Campaign Committee for our local public school board. Karen is eminently qualified to serve in the role of providing oversight and strategic guidance to the board and the administration. She provided positive, strong and independent views to the board and administrators that resulted in improved outcomes for our students and staff. Hopefully she will continue to influence our school system going forward.

Lars Hagen
Campaign Committee Member

Acknowledgements

First and foremost, I'm grateful for the opportunities the Lord has provided over the years. I've been blessed to gain the knowledge, skills, and abilities that have brought me to this point in my life. I look forward to stepping through the next open door.

I'm thankful for my lifelong partner and husband Chuck Hiltz. I wouldn't be able to write and share if it weren't for his love and support.

I must give thanks to my campaign team. They are the best, most dedicated and unwavering group I could have asked for. I'm sure I couldn't have won if it weren't for Lorie Smith, Bob Camicia, Mark Young, Darlene DeHart, Randy DeHart, Lars Hagan and Frank Chrzanowski. Thank you!

With humble gratitude I want to thank the voters in the Giles Creek District, Franklin County, VA for exercising their right to vote, voting for me, and allowing me the opportunity to serve. It's one of the experiences I'll forever remember.

Lastly, I want to thank School Board Members around the country for choosing to serve. There are many challenges, but when we are able to make improvements that support quality education, it's worth our time and effort. Though there are many who I've had the privilege of meeting during my term in office, I particularly want to thank Penny Blue, Victoria Manning and Tonya Mabe Freeman for their insights, wisdom, and common sense they have shared over the years. It truly benefits those we serve when we discuss the issues and listen to differing perspectives.

Contents

Introduction i
The Campaign and Winning the Election 1
The Apple Report 11
Vision | Leadership | A Plan 21
Who's in Charge? 30
The First Meeting 40
Transparency 49
Sharing Opinions 58
Developing the Budget 66
Data Requests 75
Accountability and Responsibility 85
The Customer 97
Doing What's Right 108
Final Thoughts 115

Introduction

How many of you have ever thought about serving on a public school board? If you are like me, I decided to run for election because I believed the experience, knowledge, and skills I brought to the table could help improve the system. Boy was I mistaken!

Starting my career as a business professional, I was introduced to the world of education and teaching later in life. During my years as a professor at the college level in Virginia, I came to the realization that the education system was failing many students. As a believer that all organizations need improvement over time, some making attempts to reinvent themselves, my teaching experiences heightened my awareness that our education system was no different than any other type of business.

In 2009 I was hired as an Assistant Professor of Business to begin the fall semester at Ferrum College, a private four-year institution, where I taught primarily upper-level undergraduate students. I made it clear on the first day of every class what the expectations were and held students accountable to those defined expectations. One of my focuses as a business professional and professor was to ensure students understood the importance of writing and making sure their documents were clear, concise, and characteristic of a business environment. I expected documents to be properly formatted and reviewed for grammar, spelling, and punctuation errors. I quickly became aware the majority of my students struggled with writing.

Being new to this environment, I initially believed it was only students in my classes who struggled, because surely not all students wrote poorly. When the spring semester started, I was disappointed to discover writing skills were below average for many students, not just those in my classes.

Pondering on writing skills, my thoughts focused on assignment papers my students submitted and what poor communicators they would be once they entered the workforce in various professional positions. Contracts would be unclear, emails would be misinterpreted, and evaluations would be incomplete or ambiguous, to name a few challenges. In addition, each of these elements would have negative financial implications to the organization.

Several years later I experienced similar problems when teaching at the masters level. Poor grammar, spelling errors, incomplete concepts, and choppy transitioning of thought were common in papers and presentations. I always provided feedback in an attempt to help students improve, but subsequent assignment submissions weren't reflective of heeding any advice or recommendations. Though fewer students were in need of remediation, I found that writing skills for students seeking an MBA didn't consistently meet my expectations.

Based on these experiences, my interests were sparked to further my own education and seek ways to help shape the future of the education system at the local and state levels, which is where significant, lasting impacts are made. Also, during the pursuit of my doctorate degree is when I became involved with serving on boards.

The first experience I had serving was in 2012 when I was asked to join a local private Christian school board. We were five members with a variety of experiences and we worked well together. Our mission was simple: Teach children to love God and do their best in whatever they did. It was a young school with no specific church affiliation and this brought with it issues the board needed to address such as funding, programs, and hiring teachers. However, in 2015 a local church took over responsibility for the school and I rotated off the board to finish my doctoral program.

Soon after rotating off the private school board several people approached me about running for the local public school board in Franklin County, VA. They believed my experience and passion for improving education would be an asset for the children in the county. I said "no" several times before I actually thought and prayed about venturing into this arena. Though I knew I had excellent qualifications, I'm a school choice advocate and thought this might not be well received. Also, I was running against an incumbent, which is often an uphill race. At the last minute I decided to take the challenge and, as you might have guessed, I actually beat the incumbent, by a wide margin. However, my campaign team deserves the majority of the credit, as their experience and wisdom helped hone and convey my message to the voters.

The election was in November 2015 with my term beginning in January 2016. Also, in the summer of 2016 I was appointed by the county supervisors to serve as the representative to the Virginia Western Community College Local Advisory Board. Based on these experiences, my position on various issues, and my passion for improving the outdated model of one-size-fits-all, I was afforded opportunities to serve on several non-profit education boards.

This book focuses on my experiences, my perceptions, and a firsthand look through my lens while serving as an elected public school board member. During the four years I spent with this group, I learned about K-12 public schools, motivations of other people, individuals who view themselves as movers and shakers, and why I chose not to seek re-election. It was also a time when I learned a lot about myself.

When I made the announcement to not seek re-election, many people asked why. I had several reasons, which the following chapters will shed some light. However, the primary response was that my husband wanted to move to a state with warmer weather and more favorable tax laws for retirees. When pressed for more information, I would simply reply, "I'm not a good fit for this board" or "This was the best, worst experience of my life." All three of these responses reflect my truth.

Politics is a tough business! Any individual who seeks to promote change within a bureaucratic government system will face a range of memorable experiences, some good and some not so good. Elected officials have the privilege of meeting and interacting with a lot of great people, which impart many rewarding experiences. However, being an independent thinker and rocking the boat presents a range of challenges. Hard lessons will be learned, long-term office holders will seek to hold on to their perceived power and control, and the status quo will be the *sacred cow* to protect.

The Campaign and Winning the Election

Initially, I wasn't willing to consider running for a public office. I knew I had good credentials, but credentials alone don't equate to winning an election. It was more about uncertainty; not being fully aware of the expectations or comprehending all that was necessary to win. After several conversations with my husband and other family members, as well as contemplating what I could bring to the team, I decided to embark on this new venture as candidate for public school board.

Building a Team

Being the novice, I had several questions to think through before deciding to venture into elected public life. I wasn't sure how much time would be necessary to do the job in a manner in which I would be proud. It was important to me that my constituents know I would be doing what I believed was best for them. What about a campaign team? Fortunately for me, a team from a previous campaign was willing to join forces to help me win.

I am grateful to each of these individuals as they brought years of experience and proficiency to the team, not only with elections in general, but with public education in particular. For example, our campaign manager was a former locally elected official extremely knowledgeable in local politics, which was a Godsend. A couple of team members had years of experience in K-12 public schools. Several were involved in local and state campaigns and held positions in political groups. Another was a sitting county supervisor. In addition, each one brought great organizational skills and was instrumental in helping me develop a winning message that correlated with what I stood for, which is critical to any undertaking.

The Apple Design

Thinking back, I remember the first meeting in June 2015. I stated I wanted an "apple" to be the shape of my campaign signs and was met with silence. It was apparent not all team members were fully on board with this idea, but I was adamant. Deciding to move forward, I located a sign company in Davenport, Iowa, who claimed they could create and produce apple-shaped yard signs. After looking at their website to see what they were capable of producing and speaking with them, my next step was to get a design draft along with a price quote. After a few iterations of reviewing the design template, we received a final quote that was within our financial means so we placed an initial order for standard yard signs. Over the course of a couple weeks we ordered pins, magnetic signs, and large signs.

Thus began the concept of *The Apple Report* where I created a Facebook (FB) page as a way to inform voters about my campaign. I posted weekly reports letting voters know where I was speaking, pictures from previous speaking engagements, answered questions, and simply used it as a tool to communicate with the public. We also worked with local publications to identify my platform issues via an ad, which stated the following:

TOGETHER We CAN Do Better! By:
- ✓ Pledging to be a dedicated steward of our tax dollars
- ✓ Being a dedicated full-time team member that will address priority issues and involve the right stakeholders (parents, teachers, tax payer, admin)
- ✓ Supporting a strategic approach to Career and Technical Education (to assist with dropout and graduation rates)
- ✓ Cultivating an environment that maximizes each student's learning potential
- ✓ Attracting and retaining high performing and motivated teachers

Along with posting on FB, the local paper agreed to print *The Apple Report* updates throughout the campaign.

Funny enough, two team members told me after the election they were initially skeptical of the apple-shaped signs because they were not typical for campaigns. One of them actually admitted it was a genius move, not that I'm a genius, because, remember, I had never run for public office and was definitely a novice. I simply picked a design – an apple – that I believed stood out, was different, and known to be affiliated with education.

The Value of Signs

A couple of team members put together a sign-placement-list in order to capitalize on visibility around the district. Of course, permission had to be obtained from the landowners, as the majority of locations were on private property. The county is decidedly rural and strategically placing signs was one of the most effective ways to introduce the public to my campaign. Yes, I spoke at various neighborhood gatherings, clubs, and community-sponsored events, but having people drive around the district and see the apple sign was the best way to introduce myself to the voters.

We put magnetic signs on our cars, which was another cost-effective way to advertise. On several occasions, people came up to me and asked if they could get a sign for their yard. One business owner stopped me in a store parking lot to tell me he owned property on a major roadway and would like me to put some signs there. Several shared with me that every time they saw an apple, they thought of me. I became known around the district as *the apple lady* and this made me realize the apple signs were definitely effective.

In addition to campaigning in the Gills Creek District, I began to educate myself with what voters considered to be the pressing issues when it came to K-12 education. I began attending the monthly scheduled school board meetings. Having served on the county Planning Commission from 2007-2012, I had already been attending county Board of Supervisors meetings for years and building positive working relationships. As the board responsible for allocating funds for the schools, I believed this to be an advantage and enhanced my credibility during the years spent cultivating these relationships.

Counting the Votes

Then came Election Day!

The Gills Creek voting district has two polling locations, which were open from 6am to 7pm. Though it would be a long day, I had a plan to physically spend blocks of time at the two locations throughout the thirteen-hour period. Also, several volunteers were scheduled to staff the two locations in support of my campaign, as well as other county seats.

Another idea I had was to pass out apples to voters after they cast their vote. So, a basket of apples was placed at each location and volunteers were instructed to offer them to voters as they came out of the polling station. Not everyone took an apple, but several mentioned they thought it was a great idea. Though it was a long day, with many hours of standing and asking voters for their vote, adrenalin was running high and I have to admit I had a lot of fun.

Once the polls closed, we headed over to the home of a friend who had graciously offered to host an election night victory party. Not sure what the results would be, as I was running against an incumbent, but we were nevertheless optimistic. The TV was on the station broadcasting the election results and several individuals had logged onto their personal devices to watch as the numbers were being reported. It doesn't take as long to tabulate for local elections, so by 9pm we knew the results. I WON! I beat the incumbent with a final vote count of 71 percent to 29 percent.

As you can imagine I was excited, to say the least, about winning my one and only election to date. Our campaign team had worked hard, tirelessly getting my message out to the public. It was not all smooth going, but we worked together in order to meet the objective, which was to achieve a win. And to beat an incumbent, I was ecstatic.

What's Next?

So many thoughts ran through my head. What were the next steps? When should I reach out to the other members to introduce myself? Who else did I need to reach out to with regards to joining the school board? I knew the issues I wanted to focus on, which incorporated strategic planning, communication with all stakeholders, budget accountability, and transparency. I believe all of these, and more, could use improvement based on what many parents, grandparents, teachers, and residents had told me during the campaign. However, I hadn't yet grasped how the system did or did not work and the processes and procedures that existed within the system.

Once the vote count was tabulated and officially finalized, I had to schedule a time to be sworn in. This could be done in a couple of ways. Newly elected officials can schedule a time to appear at the County Court House to be sworn in by the Clerk of the Court or a Judge. Or, two or more to the same board can schedule a time to meet at the respective board office and be sworn in together. I was sworn in by the Clerk of the Court.

After the election and prior to my first meeting, the assistant to the superintendent of public schools called to let me know I had to take care of a few administrative details. For example, I needed to have an official picture taken and submit it to the board clerk. In addition, I needed to have an email account created, contact the technical department to identify the type of technology I would prefer in order to access accounts and applications relevant to school board duties, and set a time to meet one-on-one with the superintendent.

Formal Orientation Training

One facet I expected was an orientation for new members, but the school division I joined didn't provide any formal orientation beyond the one-on-one with the superintendent. Thinking this unusual based on my business experience, I agreed to the meeting knowing this was a new environment I was entering. A few documents were provided such as the proposed budget for the current year, school calendar including a list of schools and principals, and a few general items. It was an informal discussion, including what I thought was minimal, general information relevant to the division and school board. Though this meeting didn't rest well with me, I would soon learn why this type of meeting was the preferred way of having a discussion. Leaving this initial interaction left me with more questions than answers. However, two documents I believed to be relevant were the division's current organizational chart and strategic plan; I requested a copy of each.

I'm a curious person and believe in making informed decisions. Therefore, I decided to research what tools and programs were available for elected officials. I knew several persons that held elected office and reached out to some of them, as well as known organizations. These contacts fell within as well as outside the school division. Through them, I became aware that the primary organization providing support is the Virginia School Board Association (VSBA), a public school lobbying entity located in Charlottesville. They offer relevant training and webinars, host an annual convention, and provide other resources for school board members throughout the state.

Taking time to review the website, I became aware of a course titled *New School Board Orientation* and decided to enroll in the session. This opportunity provided various pieces of formal documentation that included a manual, operating standards based on state legislation and statutes, and an outline of the political process regarding bills and the passage of legislation. Most important, the course offered an opportunity for networking with other board members around the state.

I was excited to become a part of this school board *team* and believed I had knowledge, skills, and experience that could be of benefit in various ways. Though I presumed I had a knowledge deficit when it came to K-12 education, I was eager and willing to learn as much as I could in order to marry my talents with improving education for all children in our division.

The Apple Report

As previously identified, the apple was the shape of my campaign signs. I wanted something different! A sign people could identity with; would recognize and remember. After all, yard signs are one of the most valuable ways to get your name out to the public. They allow people to become familiar with your campaign, and, quite frankly, to start conversations, which ended up being a winning strategy. Yes, my signs were noticed and effective!

Using Social Media

Once elected, I continued to use *The Apple Report* Facebook page to communicate with my constituents. Again, I thought this was a good idea. However, a few school board members didn't and some of my posts led to rather contentious conversations and emails.

I'm a firm believer that communication is one of the most important skills to master, yet the most difficult to sustain over any period of time. Communicating must be intentional. It requires thought, particularly when it comes to word use, as words have meaning. It requires tact, as well as honesty. It's no wonder people find it difficult to talk to each other, particularly when it requires communicating unpleasant or unwelcome information, such as declining student population or a negative encounter at the high school involving students.

I used the report to convey all types of information. This included multiple posts regarding school visits, which I made it a point to visit each school in the division at least once a year. Other posts were used to convey a variety of scheduled events being held around the division to include dates, times, and locations. Articles were shared regarding learning opportunities or notable ideas I came across in an attempt to support employees with improving styles, techniques, and classroom methods. I highlighted and discussed good ideas, tools, or programs being implemented in other divisions. An array of recognitions related to students, employees, programs, and events that occurred in any given month and throughout the year. I made every effort to highlight positive happenings that were going on in the schools and around the division.

The one constant that was posted every month was my report based on the monthly board meeting. The meetings were held on the second Monday of the month and by Wednesday I'd post the report. I sent it to the local newspaper, which graciously published the report. In addition, other Facebook pages and websites would share the report to help inform the community of what was going on within the schools.

The Not So Good

Unfortunately, not all news is good news. At times I reported on news some of the other members didn't think I should have shared. I'm one who believes the public has a right to hear the good, the bad, and the ugly, because taxpayers are providing the funding to operate the system. There was a point in time when *The Apple Report* became contentious.

Without a doubt, the first awkward encounter was in my first meeting. I would not sign a VSBA written document, which asked all Virginia school board members via their signature to oppose the proposed amendment to the Virginia constitution regarding charter schools. What I stated in the public meeting and subsequently shared in that month's issue of *The Apple Report* did not sit well with a few of the other members. The board chair interrupted me in public before I concluded my comments, a clear indication that at least one member didn't want to hear what others had to say. At that moment, I determined discussing issues wasn't the objective; it was more about controlling the agenda.

Employee Evaluations

Another issue I was vocal and wrote about was employee evaluations, which I argued should be based on performance, whether it pertained to the superintendent or any employee working within the system. As previously identified, a primary board responsibility is to hire the division superintendent, which includes providing an annual evaluation. My business experience included performance evaluations, so I thought this would be helpful to my role on the board. On second thought, maybe not!

Early in my term there was a meeting held at the Middle School where the discussion focused on revising the teacher salary scale. I brought up performance evaluations and the possibility of using a pay band model for salaries. I was adamantly informed that the education system couldn't be run like a business. Its responsibility was to educate children, not produce widgets. In addition, one administrator said they couldn't possibly do a performance evaluation because all their teachers were great and couldn't rank one over another. I admit that made me pause, given my experience and role within the system.

That meeting led me to check the VSBA training schedule to see if they offered any course that helped with understanding salary scales, maybe as part of a funding course. I didn't find anything related to salary, but I noticed an offering for a *Superintendent Evaluation Workshop*, so I signed up for the upcoming session. Since I was adamantly informed that education isn't a business, I wanted to understand what was different and what information was being conveyed via an evaluation workshop.

As with many evaluation systems in professional environments a template is utilized, to facilitate discussion between employee and employer. This primary tool is used to document goals and objectives to be met over a stated period of time. I found the workshop informative, but also was pleased to realize it had an evaluation template where identified goals and objectives were to be established.

A revelation I realized was that the superintendent evaluation form was based on performance. The guidelines are actually stated under *Part 2: Uniform Performance Standards for Superintendents* along with the standards and indicators to be used. Seven performance standards are found under *Part 5: Rating Superintendent Performance* that are to be evaluated.

Let's consider the process for the first superintendent evaluation I participated in, using the VSBA template. It began with the superintendent filling out the template, then the chair shared it with the board members, we were then asked to provide input and provide a performance ranking of either *exemplary*, *proficient*, *developing/needs improvement* or *unacceptable* on the seven standards, and ended with the chair compiling the information for final board approval. I took this seriously, so I reviewed information relevant to the standards and compared that to the superintendent's input. My feedback consisted of identifying strengths and weaknesses, commenting on the stated goals set by the superintendent, and providing recommendations. The board members discussed the evaluation and the ranking we provided, but not all input was considered or factored into the final. In my third year I didn't sign the evaluation as I couldn't sign a document that I believed to be inaccurate. The last year I wasn't even asked to sign the final.

Let's look at teacher evaluations. Having obtained relevant information and expecting consistency or at least similar concepts, I began questioning why teachers weren't given performance evaluations. From what I had seen, the typical teacher evaluation was based on classroom observations, which are subjective, and related to instructional capability and classroom management. The process required an administrator to provide input based on, quite frankly, *do they follow the rules* and *do they play well with others*. These factors may be important, but are subjective and basically not measurable from a performance perspective.

There is one measurable factor that is heavily weighted, which centers on Standards of Learning (SOL) test scores and how well students perform.

Classrooms, instructional methods, and techniques are utilized to help students consume knowledge, but a teacher can't force a child to learn, study, or pass a test. In most cases even the best teacher, who's been teaching for twenty or thirty years, has students who don't do well on tests due to a variety of factors.

This leads to the debate about salaries. How equitable are they and what justifies salary increases? Whether the discussion is focused on initial hires, retention, or from a longevity perspective, I believe an element of performance needs to be interjected. Otherwise, how can any board truly justify giving two employees the same increase when it's clear one is struggling and the other is excelling? What are increases based upon? Student SOL scores?

Student Issues

It was intentional for the board to refrain from discussions that informed the public about students and their behaviors, incidents, actions, or other events that would bring about some measure of discipline. Discussions took place, but individual cases were confined to closed session with minimal information provided during the public session, because specific legislation drives decision-making when it comes to students.

The Family Educational Rights and Privacy Act (FERPA) prohibit specific student information from being shared. There is generic reporting of data regarding students such as graduation rates, SOL scores, dropout rates, and attendance, but this information is not specific to any one student. The compiled data is used specifically for reporting to the state Department of Education for statistical purposes.

Therefore, issues involving specific student incidents and behaviors that came before the board were not discussed in *The Apple Report*.

Employee Indiscretions

I did write about employee issues, but was intentional with keeping the discussion generic. So, let's talk about employee indiscretions, which especially angered me, because these primarily related to bad behavior and poor decision-making. In any given year, news reports across the country alert the public to teachers, administrators, coaches, and other employees who have been caught crossing the line. It's not uncommon for workplaces to discover employees having affairs, drinking on the job, or participating in financial manipulations for personal gain.

In the education world teachers and administrators have been caught having inappropriate interactions and relationships with students, some sexual in nature. Some are caught hosting parties in their homes and allowing minors to indulge in alcohol and drugs, even providing the illegal substances to the minors. I find this inexcusable and reprehensible. Once proof is presented, the consequence should be, at a minimum, removal from the classroom and revocation of licensure.

So, what happens when adults are caught doing nefarious acts? Well, based on employee discipline policy and the discretion of the administration, some employees could be charged with a crime, IF someone files charges. Existing policy allowed employees who were tenured or favored by the administration to be placed on paid or unpaid administrative leave. However, based on my experience, the most common consequence for those engaged in bad behavior was simply to make the decision to allow for a *voluntary* end of the employment contract. This practice provided an escape for the division and allowed them to say they did something about the situation. On the other hand, the sad reality was it permitted the employee to move to another division and continue their bad behavior.

Protecting the reputation of the division is first and foremost when it comes to handling these types of indiscretions. Rather than hold people accountable for their actions, it's preferable to minimize the negative press and make the public believe the division is responsible by taking action to remedy the situation. I'll state that not all incidents are criminal, but many are what I'd irrefutably categorize as inappropriate or unethical. It's unfortunate that bad behavior is tolerated at the expense of protecting public perception, personal agendas, and reputations.

In my opinion, this is misplaced protection. Yes, the system should afford reasonable protections for all: it's called *due process* under the U.S. Constitution. However, it's not deemed responsible to protect adults who knowingly engage in inappropriate behavior. On the other hand, it is deemed responsible to protect students. Protections, first and foremost, should be directed towards ensuring that a safe and healthy environment is maintained for students. The system can and must do better!

Vision | Leadership | A Plan

While working on my dissertation for my doctorate, one of the interviews I conducted was with the State Superintendent of Louisiana. I was also running for school board at the time, so I took a few minutes after the interview to seek his advice. He'd been in education his entire career and I was confident he would have some pearls of wisdom to share.

The one statement that resonated with me was *vision, leadership, and a plan*. He expressed a desire to see all the divisions in the state display these three characteristics. As I've learned, some are better than others at exhibiting them, in part because boards are made up of individuals with varying agendas, biases, and experiences. I've also discovered flexibility is necessary to implement curriculum, programs, and policies in a manner that best enhance the division. On the other hand, flexibility can give way to negative outcomes, which does impact the ability to meet student needs and expectations.

Where to Begin

As I began this journey, I thought I'd start by attempting to understand how the system was organized, how it operated, and what was on the horizon. The first two documents I asked for were the organization chart and the board's strategic plan. From a business perspective, these are important foundational documents that should be reviewed and absorbed. The chart lays out organizational levels and positions of authority, which provide insight into processes and procedures, to include the reporting structure. The strategic plan conveys expectations as well as insight into the direction the organization intends to go and where it wants to be in the future. My request was met even though I was provided an outdated copy of the chart, but the second document I received was not what I would describe as a strategic plan developed at the school board level. It was a document titled *Six Year Plan* and represented an operational, not strategic, plan, which are not one in the same.

My need to learn as much as I could about how the organization worked to what was being reported led to a review of policies and budget documents, visiting schools, and talking to staff. I began to contemplate what value I would be able to offer. I thought it wise to understand where the division was predicted to be in five to ten years. What programs would be implemented? What capital improvements were being requested and over what period of time? What were the projections for student population and staff? What was the overall strategy? In my mind, all of these questions had broad implications for the future of the division and educating students.

Failure = Lesson Learned

As an imperfect person, I have many flaws and experienced many failures. However, when it comes to the school board, I believe the leadership failure I experienced and that dominates my thoughts today, was my inability to move career and technical education (CTE) forward for the students. Several years before my term began, the division realized the need for additional CTE offerings and it continued to be discussed throughout my four years.

Let me clearly state: In order to move forward with any business venture or program expansion, a plan must be developed and someone must lead the effort to accomplish the vision. This specifically means someone must be assigned to lead the program and be given the tools and resources to achieve the goals. This is a basic concept in business. It should be a basic concept in education.

I remember the first meeting I attended regarding the expansion of CTE, a few months after I took office. It was held in the school board meeting room with individuals from the business community, local community college, adult learning center, school board members, and county supervisors. They were a good mix of professionals who brought an impressive breadth of knowledge, experience, and data to the discussion. It was probably the best discussion I participated in during my term and I left hopeful that we could move forward with expanding CTE opportunities.

Unfortunately, this was the last meeting I was invited to attend. A month or so after the CTE meeting, the board chair sent an email requesting members identify what committees they wanted to serve on, because assignments would be on the agenda and made at the next meeting. I had requested to serve on the budget committee because of my experience; CTE because I believed it was desperately needed. Also, transparency and expansion of CTE had been part of my campaign. Needless to say, I was not assigned to either committee. This was the first of many signals that my knowledge and experience were not welcome.

Over my four years, I suggested and recommended we partner with local businesses for internships and apprenticeships. The county supervisors had voted to approve a business park and were negotiating with businesses to open facilities as part of the county's efforts related to economic development. This was a perfect opportunity to include in the negotiations an assurance that educational opportunities would be afforded to our students, which would benefit the businesses, community, and students seeking crucial work skills. This recommendation fell on deaf ears.

Another proposal was to consider working with adjacent divisions to consider promoting a regional CTE facility. I thought it would be good for the division to take the lead on an effort of this nature. I knew Virginia had regional governor schools and schools for the disabled, so why not for CTE? I shared that the concept was not new, because other divisions in the state were doing exactly this. School divisions and businesses to the northeast of Richmond had given a presentation at a VSBA annual convention on this very subject and shared the successes they were experiencing. The majority wasn't interested and dismissed the suggestion that this could be a viable option. Again, this went nowhere.

Missed Opportunity

Expanding CTE was one of the opportunities the division failed to consider, based on introducing a meaningful approach and yes, there were others. In my opinion, the board didn't take on a leadership role that ensured the focus would provide the pragmatic, quality education needed for 21st century students.

Take discipline; it was an ongoing issue, whether it involved disruptive behavior in the classroom or bringing a weapon to school. Policy stipulated the remedies to be utilized, but there always seemed to be the need for tolerance. Several comments I heard reiterated, depending on the case, were *He's a child* or *They have a bad home life* or *It was a mistake*. Doing nothing and appearing to be compassionate became preferable to ensuring accountability and that consequences were equitable to the incident.

For example, there were students with years of documented infractions such as poor behavior, bad grades, disrespect via actions and words to teachers and administrators, and drug violations, yet little to nothing would be done. Some violations warranted in-school suspensions (ISS) or out-of-school suspensions (OSS), but students often viewed these punishments as a way to get out of going to class. I agreed that administrators should try to manage situations before coming to the board, but disrespect and continuous poor behavior should never be tolerated.

The one action not condoned were cases involving a weapon, such as a knife, brass knuckles, or some type of firearm. However, several incidents of poor behavior were typically documented before a student was caught with a weapons violation that was reported and recorded. I'm certain taking a firm stand on discipline and not letting students continue with their inappropriate behavior would have deterred some. Let me paraphrase what one of my former colleagues stated numerous times: We shouldn't continue to tolerate disruptive classrooms in hopes of saving the disruptor. Expulsion should be the outcome as many of these students don't want to be in school anyway. I happen to agree!

Reading Program

A particular reading program was utilized in the majority of the elementary schools, which I was told helped many children improve their skills. I decided to visit a school and sit in on a lesson. What I witnessed was a teacher at the front of the room, using a whiteboard and a whistle, while children sat on an area rug. Of course, visitors are a bit of a distraction, so keeping the children's attention was a little more of a challenge at the moment. Anyone who has visited a 1st or 2nd grade classroom knows holding children's attention can be difficult, given the best of circumstances.

After this first visit I was asked what I thought about the reading program. Being one to express what I actually think, I said it was sad to see the children being told to sit still, listen to a teacher give a lesson for an extended period of time, and have the teacher blow a whistle to keep them focused. I deemed it rather Pavlov-ian and unnatural from a learning perspective for that age group.

On another occasion, I had the opportunity to speak with the superintendent after another school visit, where I mentioned the name of the program and said I believe it's an oxymoron. Regardless of what I thought, that fact is some of our elementary schools continued to report poor test scores and the proposed remedy was to increase the number of reading coaches. Though I expressed my opinions regarding the program early in my term and voiced concerns about the amount of funds expended annually on the program, it wasn't until my last board meeting that the division proposed introducing a new reading program. I pray the children are being better served and their reading skills are actually improving.

Necessary to Succeed

The world of education presents a multitude of factors to consider. These factors are based on needs that include facilities, curriculum, skilled employees, and parental engagement, to name a few. It takes strong leadership with a vision that's able to connect the dots and provide viable and affordable solutions.

Unless leadership is willing to convey the vision and a plan for where they intend to go, organizations will remain mediocre and flounder. Schools will continue to provide questionable quality education, which is not what parents expect or what state constitutions guarantee. Those in charge will simply maintain the status quo, which is an attempt to preserve the existing system and a bureaucracy that negates accountability.

I believe God named mankind correctly – sheep! Unfortunately, there are far too many sheep and not enough shepherds.

Who's in Charge?

The Franklin County School Board, located in southwest Virginia, consists of eight elected officials, the superintendent, assistant superintendent, clerk, and two student representatives. The elected officials are voting members, while the others are non-voting participants.

As a newly elected public official I had officially attended one school board meeting and knew who sat on the board, but I was not sure of the roles each played or the level of authority each had. The division superintendent and the chair were the ones who appeared to be in charge, but I sought further understanding. It didn't seem reasonable or appropriate that a non-voting member, the division superintendent, would frequently take the lead on the board. In addition, the chair was moving the agenda forward with little to no time for discussion of the agenda items. As a business professional, I knew this wasn't how meetings were typically conducted; as an elected official I was not comfortable with having my questions go unanswered or my comments cut short.

Training Opportunities

Personally, I needed more information. It was important for me to understand the new role and responsibilities to which I, as an elected school board member, would be held accountable. I gained an opportunity to enhance my knowledge for this new role once I discovered the Virginia School Board Association (VSBA). As it is the primary organizational provider of training courses for Virginia school board members, all board members are encouraged to take courses through this organization, though not all members partake. After all, we are in the business of education.

There's a range of offerings. The one relating to my new situation included the *Orientation for New Board Members*, a biannual course. I immediately registered for the upcoming session and was provided a variety of material, which included the manual titled *Virginia School Board – A Manual for Virginia School Board Members*. This publication is one of the more important books to digest, as it spelled out how a board is to operate and aligns with the Code of Virginia, Title 22, which is the code title that pertains to education policy.

Members and Their Role

So, what is the role of a public school board member in Virginia? How do the duties of the chair compare to the other members? In the Code of Virginia under *Title 22.1 Education, Chapter 7 General Powers and Duties of School Boards, § 22.1-79 Powers and duties* there are ten duties identified. None of the duties stipulate any member has authority over another. In fact, *§22.1-71 School board constitutes body corporate; corporate powers* articulates the following:

> *"The duly appointed or elected members shall constitute the school board. Every such school board is declared a body corporate and, in its corporate capacity, is vested with all the powers and charged with all the duties, obligations and responsibilities imposed upon school boards by law and may sue, be sued, contract, be contracted with and, in accordance with the provisions of this title, purchase, take, hold, lease and convey school property, both real and personal. School board members appointed or elected by district or otherwise shall have no organization or duties except such as may be assigned to them by the school board as a whole."*

However, the one duty the chair does have is to run the meeting in accordance with Robert's Rules of Order. ALL members have authority to request items be placed on the agenda, initiate discussion, and cast their ONE vote.

The Manual

This book consists of an introduction and twelve chapters. First, let's consider the introduction and chapter 1 as they provide a summary of the history and background regarding the organizational structure of the education system in Virginia. They identify what the Virginia constitution says about education, under Article VIII, as well as the various bodies expected to work together in order to fulfill legal obligations for providing a quality education, a guarantee under the constitution.

However, my attention was drawn to *Chapter 2 – The School Board*. This chapter speaks of the statutory elements regarding the board that I wanted to know more about, including powers, duties, membership, and ethics.

The *Powers* section states, "broad powers and great authority rest in the school board *as a unit* and no part of them rests in any member as an individual. *The school board member as an individual has no official power*" (emphasis added). This was important information as far as I was concerned, particularly in light of how I was treated in the January 2016 meeting, which is discussed in the chapter titled "The First Meeting."

Chapter 2 also states that duties fall under three categories specific to the local school board, which are to:

1. adopt policies for the school system;
2. provide adequate means of executing them; and
3. see that they are executed.

Details of specific duties based on these three categories are found in the state statutes and the *Regulations of the Board of Education*.

Board Duties

The first duty that piqued my interest was to appoint the division's superintendent of schools. This is asserted as the most important duty, because the board's decision will determine the success or failure of the division. In addition, this duty unambiguously implies the superintendent works for the school board, because the board has the responsibility to select and vote on the individual for the position. Also, the organizational chart clearly places the board at the top with the superintendent in the block under the board. This reflects chain of command, using a military term.

I would say the most troubling aspect, based on my experience, was the relationship between the superintendent and the board members. Too many superintendents act or operate as if the board *works for* and *reports to* them. In reality, the board is the final authority from a fiduciary responsibility, as well as an operational perspective. When a program doesn't work well or a negative incident occurs, the public typically reaches out to the elected officials, which is what's to be expected, in my opinion. But, without clear policy that includes processes and procedures, a strategic plan, and a willingness to work together, it's difficult to realize success and provide that desired quality education the constitution guarantees.

Another duty to highlight is the division's responsibility to present the school's needs to the body that appropriates the requested funding. In Virginia, school boards don't have taxing authority. They make their funding requests known to the county Board of Supervisors. This body has taxing authority, is the fiscal authority for the county, and allocates funding to the schools.

Let me interject here that some school divisions understand the need to hire business professionals for business positions, but that was not the case in my experience. The tendency was to hire from within, which meant promoting a teacher or administrator to serve as the Director of Human Resources or Director of Technology. My belief is this practice poses a problem in that the learning curve can be quite steep, as these individuals do not typically have the skill sets for the job.

Hiring internal employees simply promotes the status quo. So, when it comes time to develop the budget to request funding from the supervisors, I had little confidence in the projected numbers. In addition, when proposed budgets are presented in a confusing manner with limited data to support the array of requested items, this doesn't instill confidence or promote positive working relationships. The quality of working relationships is critical for any organization to move forward with any requests, whether they are budget, program, or system oriented.

The last duty I'll highlight is receiving and acting on written and oral communications from citizens, as well as employees and external organizations. On many occasions during my term, emails or entries entered in the anonymous suggestion box were not addressed, at least to my knowledge. When a particular piece of communication would be brought up in the public meeting or sent directly to board members, it was common for the superintendent to claim it was taken care of. However, on more than one occasion it was identified that the individual was not satisfied with the proposed solution regarding the incident or the resolution imposed.

In addition, it needs to be formally documented. One example would be to add a column to the right of the suggestions box spreadsheet that identifies the action taken along with the date. Either way, my belief is any issue raised, particularly when it impacts multiple schools, students, or the public, should be brought to the attention of all board members, not just one or two.

There were occasions when I was blindsided by an issue because information wasn't shared with all members. For example, I had a constituent Facebook message me to inquire about a letter they had received from the Office of the Assistant Superintendent. It was an inquiry asking what this letter was about and should they respond. I was not aware this correspondence was going out to certain parents within the division or the purpose of the communication. I immediately emailed the Assistant Superintendent to request answers and obtain relevant information so I could intelligently inform my constituent. From my perspective, this not only indicated poor communication, but disrespect as well as a lack of leadership.

Board Culture

Ethics and the *Code of Ethics* are the last two sections in chapter 2. I would argue these were regularly ignored by several of the board members I served with. First, the code clearly states policy decisions should only be made after *full discussion* is finished at publicly held board meetings. My first meeting showed me that full discussion wasn't always a consideration or even welcome.

Second, the code states the board's first and greatest concern must be the educational welfare of the students attending the public schools. Well, I will undoubtedly state that I don't believe all decisions made and all votes taken were always with this concern in mind. Too often decisions were made for political expediency, to protect employees, or to advance a particular agenda. If students were the focus, then teachers would be fired, policy would be applied consistently, useful and relevant data would be provided, and the budget would be completely transparent. After all, the taxpayer funds the public education system; it's the duty of the board to keep them informed.

Attending this course confirmed in my mind the board is the leadership. They are responsible and accountable for developing strategy, defining goals, and helping guide the team in the direction that enables achieving success. However, several meetings later I continued to leave asking myself, "Who's in charge of the division?" and "Why does the board seem to subjugate their responsibilities to the superintendent?" My sense led me to surmise that board members lacked knowledge and understanding regarding the role they play and the leadership they are expected to provide.

Final Answer

People elect individuals they believe will work together, formulate strategies, obtain realistic goals that are financially feasible, advance practical outcomes, and do their best to ensure quality education is provided to all students.

Decisions should be based on the will of the people and to do what is best for the majority. When officials ignore constituents, make poor decisions, and consider self above all else, they lose trust.

So who's in charge? I'll tell you it's not the superintendent. Running a school division is a team sport, which includes elected officials and hired staff. However, the elected members are the leadership. They are the ones responsible for being the change agents that drive strategy, goals, and direction. They are the persons who have fiduciary responsibility for appropriated funds. They are the ones who answer to the taxpayer. They are the ones in charge!

The First Meeting

While driving to my first school board meeting, held monthly in Rocky Mount, VA, I told myself I'd sit back for the first several meetings and do my best to listen and learn. Well, you know what they say about best-laid plans!

January 11, 2016 was my first meeting as an elected school board member. It was also the month when the Virginia General Assembly began its legislative session. Various bills had been filed and were being introduced, discussed, and amended by the respective committees and subcommittees. Several proposed bills were introduced that dealt with education, but three specific ones dealt with charter schools. I happen to agree with what was being proposed and thought they would benefit children. However, particular attention was given to these bills by the VSBA. Not initially familiar with protocol and processes, I wasn't aware VSBA had already begun organizing and reaching out to the 133 school divisions throughout the state in order to aid in the defeat of charter school authority and expansion.

Proposed Legislation

The proposed legislation consisted of one Senate bill (SB 588) and two joint resolutions (HJ 1 and SJ 6). These proposals introduced a state Constitutional Amendment regarding charter schools. Virginia requires two consecutive years of passage in the house and senate in order to incorporate a constitutional amendment. Therefore, the joint resolutions needed to be introduced in the 2016 session, which was the second year.

The House Joint Resolution (HJ1) stated:

"Grants the Board of Education authority, subject to criteria and conditions prescribed by the General Assembly, to establish charter schools within the school divisions of the Commonwealth. This is the second resolution for Senate Joint Resolution 256 (2015)."

The Senate Joint Resolution (SJ1) stated:

"Grants the Board of Education authority, subject to criteria and conditions prescribed by the General Assembly, to establish charter schools within the school divisions of the Commonwealth."

Both resolutions failed in their respective chambers.

Simply put, the primary purpose of the joint resolutions was to allow the Virginia State Board of Education to have authority to approve charter schools. Though the state board reviews charter applications, the current language leaves approval authority to the local school board. I view this to be a conflict of interest in that local boards don't want competition. This is why approving and allowing a charter school to be within any particular division was and remains unacceptable, as reflected by the low number of charters in VA.

Senate Bill 588 was introduced in the 2016 general assembly session by Senators David R. Suetterlein and Mark D. Obenshain. Senator Suetterlein was my state Senator, with whom I had several conversations on this issue. Also, I was given an opportunity to speak with Senator Obenshain about this bill at an earlier local event. The bill summary states:

"Provides for a referendum at the November 8, 2016, election to approve or reject an amendment to grant the Board of Education the authority to establish charter schools within the school divisions of the Commonwealth, subject to any criteria or conditions that the General Assembly may prescribe."

In my opinion, it seemed reasonable to allow voters to decide whether or not they wanted to increase the number of charter schools within the state. Unfortunately, the vote resulted in the following:

"SB 588 – Constitutional Amendment (voter referendum); charter schools. Introduced by David R. Suetterlein | Mark D. Obenshain. Senate vote 20 to 20, which resulted in Chair votes No, bill defeated on 2/15/16. This bill would have allowed a referendum on Nov 8, 2016."

For those who aren't quite sure what a charter school is, they are part of the public school system. Some will refer to private charter schools, but this is misleading. A private school is a private school, regardless of their association and how they operate. But, public charter schools share three primary components, which are:
1. they operate based on a negotiated charter,
2. they are given flexibility regarding curriculum, and
3. they are funded with tax dollars.

Virginia passed legislation in 1998 and codified it in state code, which authorizes charter schools. But, local school boards generally oppose approving charter applications. I believe the VSBA lobbying efforts reflect this as well. As a result, only eight charter schools are operating in the state, which is extremely low compared to surrounding states with charter authority.

For example, the Maryland Alliance of Public Charter Schools identifies 50 and the North Carolina Center for Public Policy Research identifies 184 operating charters in 2020. In addition, the U.S. Department of Education reports that 6,900 operate nationally as of May 2016 and yet Virginia has eight! I will continue to conclude there is resistance from the local school boards.

I digress; let's get back to the proposed legislation. The process to open a charter school is not the same in every state because each state operates based on its own constitution and code or statutes. However, the process in Virginia requires the state board to review the application and provide a recommendation. Then the local public school board reviews and approves or denies the application to operate a charter within the division. This process poses several challenges, which I believe boils down to competition and funding. What I believe the amendment was attempting to accomplish was to give the state board approval authority as well.

School divisions claim that if they approve a charter, funding will be negatively impacted. This perception focuses on charters, but is perpetuated by those who don't want any type of education choice. Reality is the reduction in student population is what has a negative impact on funding.

Charters are public schools, funding is guided by state legislation, and allocation is based on the negotiated charter. For example, if the per pupil cost is $10,000 and the charter funding is at 70%, then $7000 is transferred from the public school to the charter school. In essence this provides a $3,000 savings to the taxpayer or it may remain within the public school system.

I do want to make it clear that not all states calculate costs the same. Funding is allocated based on state legislation and negotiated charters. However, the proposed legislation in Virginia was to amend the constitution to allow the Virginia State Board of Education approval authority for charter school applications and not leave sole authority to local school boards.

The Charter Resolution

Upon arrival at the meeting, I walked in, looked around, and noticed the seating arrangement. Mainly looking for the seat I would occupy on the dais. Having attended the previous six months of meetings, the seating arrangement seemed innocuous. Being a new member, I wasn't fully cognizant of the relationships or the politics.

The meeting was called to order, introductions were made for newly elected members, and then the chair began addressing the agenda items. The meetings are public, so several people were sitting in the audience. Little did I realize at the time the majority of the people were employees from the school division, mostly persons in administration positions who were there to give presentations, address questions, or provide additional forms of support.

We progressed through the agenda, with the majority of items being routine. These included reciting the Pledge of Allegiance; time for public comments; as well as approval of the agenda and the previous month's minutes, monthly financials, and personnel actions. Moving into New Business led to discussions on several items, including the last agenda item: *7.09: Review and consider approval of the Charter School Constitutional Amendment Resolution.*

As previously stated, the document discussed was drafted by the VSBA and sent to each of the 133 school divisions. It was designed to be a January meeting discussion, with the expectation that all school board members would agree with it and sign. Being familiar with the legislation this document addressed, but not agreeing with the resolution language, I couldn't sit back quietly and keep my mouth shut. I began to share my thoughts and opinions regarding the document, the legislation, and what it would mean to sign the resolution.

Having personally spoken with Senator Obenshain about the constitutional amendment legislation, I began to disclose some of the conversation. I stated my opinion that charter schools were a positive for many children and were similar to sending children to a governor's school, magnet school, or regional school for children with disabilities. While I was sharing my comments, the board chair interrupted me, stating it was inappropriate to discuss my conversation with Senator Obenshain and directed me to refrain from interjecting his name into the discussion. I was taken aback! I admit I wasn't fully cognizant of what was actually transpiring. The true intent of the chair, based on my perception, would be revealed over the next several months.

Vote My Conscience

The discussion ended and the resolution was passed down the line for signatures. I chose not to sign the document, because I believed the charter school process was biased. A review of the Virginia Department of Education website identifies documentation that reveals charter school applications had met criteria and were recommended by the state Board of Education for approval. However, when the package was presented to the local school board, approvals were either denied or pending.

A week after the school board meeting I had the opportunity to travel to Richmond to visit several Delegates and Senators. Stopping at the office of Senator Suetterlein, co-sponsor of SB 588 bill, I sought his perspective as to how he thought the vote count would go. Pass or fall short? Seeing me, he immediately pulled out a piece of paper from a drawer, which was the resolution. He expressed he was pleased to see that I stood my ground and didn't sign the document.

Transparency

I campaigned on transparency because I believe transparency was and is a responsibility from all levels of government. The public should hold officials accountable by ensuring that data and information they are providing is current, relevant, and factual. In addition, transparency needed to be a major platform issue given what I was hearing from constituents. After all, public dollars fund public education and many taxpayers are interested in knowing what the system is providing, how they can help, and how their tax dollars are being spent.

As someone who wants to see data and tries to understand what's happening over any given period of time, I found myself continually asking for supporting data. I soon realized the information provided was a *snapshot in time* regarding various programs and were basically data points that met minimum mandatory reporting requirements by the state. Typical examples included the monthly Average Daily Membership (ADM) and revenue and expenditure reports. Annual reporting statistics included

Standards of Learning (SOL) scores, graduation rates, dropout rates, and discipline. It was my opinion that the board should be provided, at a minimum, data that covered a five-year period so the decisions made would be based on informed, data-driven information and provide rationale for the decisions made. This is what I expected, but not what I experienced.

My Ally

One of my board colleagues, Ms. Penny Blue, had a similar background. We both had careers and gained experience within business environments. Mine was in the public sector; Ms. Blue's was in the private sector. Though we weren't ideologically aligned, this factor led to the positive working relationship we developed as we spoke a similar language and knew that in order for any organization, public or private, to improve, decisions needed to be based on supporting data.

The *health* of the division was a term frequently used by Ms. Blue to try to clarify the reason both of us were seeking multiple years' worth of data. We believed it was necessary in order to understand how the division was doing over time based on month-to-month and year-to-year reporting cycles. This made sense to me, but apparently it was a bridge too far for other members and the administration.

A couple of reasons I have this perspective regarding some of my former colleagues focuses on what I consider a lack of understanding when it comes to implementing best business practices as well as a lack of training.

Unfunded Requests

When it came to budget issues, one that kept rearing its ugly head was unfunded requests. The one that sticks out most in my mind is hiring personnel. I questioned the reasons why the administration found it necessary to hire new employees for new positions once the budget had been approved. I understood the need to replace an employee who left, but creating new positions? Shouldn't that have been part of the planning process?

Anyway, my experience includes years of working with budgets and evaluating cost proposals for large federal programs. Employees or full-time equivalents (FTE) are identified and requested during budget development based on the program, along with certain identified circumstances or situations. Hiring FTEs once the budget has been approved is not meant to be automatic or easy. I realize there is the occasional exception, but I was concerned from a planning and funding perspective when requests for new FTE's were occurring annually.

I would invariably ask why the division needed a new FTE and did we have the funds to pay the salary? The typical response was the position was needed for some arbitrary reason, but we weren't necessarily provided written or supporting documentation explaining why. Funds were always available, even though the position wasn't identified until after the budget was approved. I'm not quite sure how that works other than to make the presumption that proposed funds needed to cover annual salaries were estimated. Regarding some of the new hires or increases in salaries, one response was to use Title funds, which are authorized under certain federally funded programs. But, these funds are typically identified up front based on ADM.

In accordance with generally accepted accounting practices (GAAP), once a budget is approved there are limited reasons to move funding as each dollar is appropriated for a specific purpose or use. Some transfers require going back to the funding source for approval, as all transfers must be in compliance with appropriation law.

After the first couple of new FTE requests, I became more concerned and asked for detailed financial information. The financials provided to the board with high-level, not line item-level, reporting. Unfortunately, during my tenure we were never presented budget allocations by school, central office, board duties, operations, or program. The most common responses were something like: "We have a new accounting system and need time to produce detailed reports" or the chair would say we don't need the detail;

we can trust the administration. Well, my response is none of those answers negate the board's fiduciary responsibilities.

Not satisfied with what I was being told and knowing how government operates, my thoughts migrated towards the obvious as in the budget is inflated. This is not uncommon in the public or private sector, but how much wiggle room is the question. Salaries are the largest expenditure for a school division and I wouldn't expect too much excess in that line item.

Closed Session

There were other issues where I believe transparency was lacking. One of the more heartbreaking was inappropriate or criminal behavior towards students. Though it wasn't a monthly issue, it was an annual issue and was always reserved for discussion during closed session. The Code of Virginia, §2.2-3711 Closed meetings authorized for certain limited purposes, provides 54 reasons for what is authorized to be discussed in closed versus open session. I'm not sure I would agree that 54 meets the definition of limited purposes, but discussions involving certain elements related to employees were reserved for closed session.

I'm of the mind that school employees are public employees and, therefore, issues concerning them should be discussed during public session. However, I appreciate the constitutional right of innocent until proven guilty and the need to substantiate allegations and refrain from discussing pending court cases. There is the need to handle sensitive information responsibly. On the other hand, when I'm informed of inappropriate behavior regarding an employee based on a newspaper article, it's become part of the public domain. If questions arise, then the board should publicly share what they can or simply state it's an ongoing case and is not privy to public discussion at this time. The board shouldn't be obligated to protect tenured or favored employees.

It's appropriate to be respectful of fairness, liability, slander, and other perceived harms that may fall on an employee. However, it's also appropriate to ask why an employee should get away with harming a child they are expected to teach and protect. Who is paying their salary? Don't parents have a right to know who is teaching their children?

I'm aware of inappropriate behavior and poor choices made by public school employees within the division I served as well as other divisions around the state. One doesn't have to dig too far to read articles from around the country about misappropriation of funds, falsifying test scores, alcohol and drug use, or sexual misconduct. Unfortunately, if the case doesn't make its way to the press, more often than not the employee is given a choice: resign or be fired. Guess which option is taken?

Abuse and bullying don't happen only in the home or between children. It happens between people of all ages. Though all actions aren't criminal, decisions are made that should anger all of us. Bad character is revealed based on poor decision-making and the use of social media shaming, which do take place in all schools, among all ages.

Public Session

In one of my *Apple Reports* I wrote about the need for transparency; the next month's public meeting led to a discussion focused on whether the division was transparent or not. At the end of each meeting, board members are given an opportunity to bring up any other issues not included on the agenda. This is when the chair decided to bring up the topic of transparency *and* specifically requested the other board members to share their thoughts. I wasn't surprised it was brought up, because I'd written about the subject the previous month.

One member and long-time county resident immediately spoke up and clearly stated that the division was very transparent. I waited until the others had weighed in and then I shared my opinion, which reiterated what I addressed in the report. The chair asked me what the division was not transparent about. I rattled off a list, including budget, curriculum, data, and programs, to name a few. I further articulated my reasons why I didn't believe there was transparency regarding these items, with the most obvious reason being the lack of data the board receives. This ended the discussion and the meeting was closed.

In my heart I believe this was brought up in an attempt to embarrass me during the public session. The majority of the others agreed with the chair or said nothing. I believe only two other members spoke up to make a public comment. This was not the first, nor was it the last time the chair addressed me in a condescending tone or challenged my opinions. This behavior merely emboldened me to speak what I believe to be the truth. It inspired me to be a voice for the voiceless. This was a defining point in time when I began to be intentional, yet respectful, about discussing issues during public session. I was determined I wouldn't be bullied, shamed, or belittled by anyone, especially someone I had little respect for.

I must share a message I was sent by a former colleague when I was teaching at the undergraduate level. An assignment she required of her students was to keep a journal and report about various meetings and events they attended and provide their input as it related to the course. While reviewing one particular journal entry, she found the student had attended a school board meeting in the spring of 2018. The entry she relayed to me was the following:

"One of my students went to a school board meeting in March or April, I can't remember when. In her journal, she wrote why are all of these men so intimidated by you? She was outraged as to how you were treated and basically came to the conclusion that your IQ is larger than theirs combined and I had to chuckle."

My response was:

"LOL!!! Appreciate you sharing. Good to get feedback, especially positive. Guess I can say 'out of the mouths of babes.'"

Now, I'm not sure what my IQ is or anyone else's, but for a student to write this in their assignment, this clearly reflects that others could see how some members treated other members. I guess there was some transparency after all!

Shining a light on various issues the taxpayers are funding is the only way the public will achieve transparency. It's up to *we the people*, the citizens, parents, and grandparents, to push back. It's up to us to demand accountability and hold public officials and employees responsible for what's happening within the public schools. If something isn't transparent, then speak up and speak out. The *silent majority* can't afford to be silent any longer!

Sharing Opinions

Anyone who has ever had a conversation with me knows when I'm asked my opinion – I freely give. It wasn't long before other board members learned I engaged by sharing my opinions along with ideas, recommendations, and suggestions. I'm a firm believer that every organization can improve by identifying the areas where improvements need to be made and figuring out how best to tackle them. From the beginning, first and foremost, my intent was to discuss and reach solutions regarding issues where the division knew it was struggling, but didn't necessarily want to publicly admit it.

What I Learned
Every board member always brings different experiences to the team with some having a broader perspective than others. It's correct to say not everyone on the board shared my perspective, nor did I expect them to. However, I did expect the opportunity to have a voice. It became apparent early on that what I said and the information I offered were not welcome. The experiences I brought to the board was viewed as

irrelevant, not a factor to consider, or didn't matter to the majority. One member told me I couldn't possibly understand or know what the division needed, because I wasn't from Franklin County. Talk about a bubble busting moment!

I vividly remember a discussion in the office of the superintendent that focused on my willingness to share my opinions, recommendations, and suggestions. At one point the superintendent stated, "There are some very smart people in this county." It was a statement I didn't expect and I'm sure a shocked look appeared on my face. It's amazing what one can learn from body language and my face typically says a lot. At that point, I stated I was very well aware of this fact. I represent an area of the county where many retirees from all walks of life reside and I can unequivocally say there are some very smart people. They include individuals who are retired military, entrepreneurs, corporate executives, famous authors, professional sports figures, and government executives, like myself. Many have worked and lived in various countries around the world and gained a wealth of knowledge and experience. On the flip side, there are families that have lived in the area for generations with quite an impressive ancestry. Some families date back to the 1600s and 1700s. So, I stated, "Yes, we do have some very intelligent, prominent people living in the county."

As the conversation progressed, it became evident that expressing my opinions, recommendations, and suggestions wasn't welcome. What I considered as helping was being interpreted as telling others what they should do versus accepting it for what it was – *simply an opinion*. My intention was meant to encourage dialogue on any given issue, not tell others what to do or how to think. Personally, I find that discussion of issues furthers my understanding as to where other members are coming from and should give all of us insight into thought processes as it relates to decision making. Hearing their considerations and experiences, how they relate to issues, and whether they have an opinion, I believe, is the difference between making a good or bad decision.

In addition, discussing the various subjects would inevitably build and promote positive working relationships within our team. Most professionals know how important it is to establish a cohesive team and relationships are a primary aspect of team building. For this particular team, team building did not appear to be an objective. Actually, it seemed the primary objective was to ensure new board members understand the party line, which was to get and stay in line.

Value of Sharing

It's interesting that networking and the ability to share is one of the most sought after opportunities in education. Many teachers and administrators ask questions and seek advice from colleagues, from both inside and outside the division. Communicating information and learning from each other is valuable in so many ways and on so many levels.

I believe this to be the primary focus of state school board associations. Each state has an education organization that hosts an annual convention. A wide range of education topics are discussed by various consultants, contractors, professionals, and employees representing various programs implemented within their divisions. This forum consisted of discussion panels, keynote speakers, and simply gathering with colleagues to discuss various sessions over lunch.

I looked forward to the convention every year because members from divisions around the state were represented. For me, the event always offered a few interesting topics and introduced a variety of creative concepts to handle particular education challenges. I attended sessions of interest to me and ones I thought our division could potentially derive benefit from. After all, schools are expected to provide students with opportunities, programs, tools, and the support necessary to ensure their constitutionally guaranteed quality education.

Strategic Thinking

It's great to bring back ideas from the conference, but unless boards have a strategy for the division's future, ideas are just that – ideas. Not only is it important to be able to incorporate new, relevant programs, but also one must think about how programs relate to the division's strategy, which is the framework for developing a plan. The plan becomes the roadmap to move forward with program implementation along with allocation of funds and resources. This is where the board will rely on the administration, through their support with research, follow-up, and reporting outcomes on a regular basis.

Boards hold fiduciary responsibility and this renders them accountable for determining the viability of concepts and programs, in addition to ensuring state-mandated and student needs are met. Discussions should center on feasibility and affordability in order to determine if there is adequate personnel and whether existing facilities are sufficient to house a particular program. Also, will there be enough student participation to make it cost-effective.

It's good to be enlightened and to have doors open that many would never consider walking through. However, just because a program sounds good doesn't mean it will be a good fit. Before trying to implement a program, it's important to review the division's strategy and make sure it's doable. Also, it's essential to remove unsuccessful programs. Choosing to walk through that open door as well as removing unsuccessful programs requires change, and change is difficult for the majority.

Networking Opportunities

I utilized two avenues to network: training opportunities and *The Apple Report* Facebook page. At the training sessions I attended, inevitably I would connect with someone based on the discussions, both topical and opinion. It was common to exchange contact information by the end of the day. Because of these relationships I cultivated, it would not be uncommon to have board members from other divisions call to discuss a scenario or specific situation they were grappling with. In turn, I reached out to others to seek advice or to learn how another division was handling a specific situation. These networking opportunities are one of the greatest benefits of being an elected school board member, from my perspective. While all divisions have similarities, each one has its own unique culture, challenges, situations, and not to mention, personalities.

Some of the discussions focused on personnel concerns, student dress code policy, or how one might handle a particular scenario. One particular subject was undertaking appropriate consequences for employees who do harm or are caught doing nefarious acts with students. This is one area I have little tolerance for and would strongly share my opinions. However, the majority of the discussions focused on what other members or superintendents were saying or doing and what decisions they were making on various issues. The advice I gave focused on my thoughts and was based on my knowledge and experience, which guided me as to how I handled any situation or vote, given the particulars.

I recall a member from another division called to ask if I was going to attend a specific training session hosted by the VSBA. I responded in the affirmative. The member stated that they would like to attend, as it appears to be a good session, but they were still contemplating because the course and travel expenses would be out of pocket. I was confused by this remark; training I attended was paid for by the division, including allowable travel expenses. I couldn't comprehend any division not doing the same for their board members. I can understand the need to limit the number of training sessions per year per board member, but telling those who are elected to make informed decisions that training is not important is the wrong message to send. I find it inconceivable that any division would not allocate funds to ensure board members know what their responsibilities are and the execution of their authority is performed in an ethical and judicious manner. On the other hand, ignorance breeds status quo.

To be an effective public servant, skills must be honed and knowledge obtained. Members should participate in relevant training and networking, but not all do. These opportunities help improve communication skills, which are a critical factor. Improving skills encourages the sharing of opinions, recommendations, and suggestions, but not many engage. This begs the question: What value are we providing to our constituents?

Being a public servant is not only an honor; it's a humbling experience. Being an informed public servant is critical to representing one's constituents.

Developing the Budget

Having retired from federal procurement where I worked with large program teams, I was familiar with budgets and the accountability associated with appropriating public funds. This is a strength I brought to the table. As a Contracting Officer for various federal departments, my experiences taught me to take the fiduciary responsibility seriously when it came to spending public funds. These opportunities furnished me with the knowledge and skills necessary to be effective in the area of understanding budget development along with expenditures involving taxpayer dollars.

One Process
Budgets are typically constructed based on a defined process. The division I served used what I'll refer to as a three-phased process. It began with the various departments and groups in the division coming in and giving presentations. Some simply submitted a sheet of paper that stated what they would like to have. The representatives

included people speaking for teachers, school administrators, bus drivers, facilities maintenance, technology, nurses, food services, and more.

Sitting through the process over multiple years taught me to expect two assertions: a need for pay raises and more personnel. However, most of the presentations didn't provide justification for either of these requested needs. They simply stated they'd not had a pay raise in several years and employee retention would be helped if employees were paid more. A few groups did comparisons with like positions in surrounding divisions, but the majority simply made the request.

Not once did I see any justification based on performance that demonstrated employees exceeded normal duties. It was frequently stated that employees were good workers, deserved more pay, and went above and beyond, but nothing was presented that I believed substantiated those claims. Also, I found it ironic that each year there was a stated need for more personnel when our student population continued to decline. There is a direct correlation between the two!

The second step involved the Finance Officer putting together a spreadsheet that included columns reflecting estimated amounts for target, high, low, and the previous year's approved budget. The numbers were based on the expected streams of funding and where they were coming from, mainly local and state government with a small percentage coming from the federal government. Once drafted, the spreadsheet was presented to the school board in a public meeting. It consisted of a list of known expenses along with a wish list put forward by the superintendent. Some of these were stated as *nice to haves*, if the funding was available.

Lists were categorical in nature, with limited supporting documentation that gave clarification or explanation as to why an item was estimated at the given cost. When supporting information was provided, it was high level with minimal detail. For example, a need for a new education program would be identified. Information from the website would be provided, but it would not be clear what the total costs would be, if they were recurring or not, and what program would be replaced, if any. Actually, I'm not sure we ever replaced anything; merely added.

Seeking competition for cost comparison was always a factor from my perspective. Not having any made me question the reasonableness of proposed costs. It was common practice for me to ask if research had been performed in order to know what other programs were available, could they be useful to student learning, and what were the associated costs. This proposed spreadsheet was the first depiction given to the board, which was meant to provide some sense of understanding related to professed necessary resources and any capital projects the division was seeking to undertake.

The final phase of the process was to present the proposed budget publicly to the Board of Supervisors, the governing body that allocates funds to the schools. After what generally resulted in a few discussions with possibly one or two joint meetings, the supervisors voted to approve a specified annual amount.

I must point out that most local public meetings had minimal attendance based on a variety of reasons. The few times I do recall seeing large audiences were when community leaders, who were issue driven, organized like-minded citizens together to attend meetings. But, typically attendance was pretty sparse. This irritated me from the perspective that votes were being cast regarding the allocation of our tax dollars with little to no public input. Yes, there would be individuals that sent emails or wrote letters, but speaking in the public square is where voices can be heard. I will say, though many don't participate in the process, there are those who will freely complain when something isn't to their liking.

Flawed Process

I found the budget process used by the division lacking. First, working sessions were minimal or not scheduled, which would allow board members to come together to discuss the various requests and establish the expectations for the division. When there was a scheduled working session, typically less than half the board participated. However, without a strategic plan there is no accountability, so this was no surprise. Funding decisions are one of the most important votes a board member casts. It's critical to understand where we've been, where we are, and where we expect to go and that's what a plan supports. Having a transparent budget process that drills down to the line item level and aligns with a plan is one of the most methodical and practical ways of building trust and having accountability. The budget, along with supporting documentation, should clearly identify funds being allocated to any given unit and for what purpose.

There were times when I would ask questions and make inquiries related to budget increases and being the detail-oriented person I am didn't necessarily serve me well. As previously stated, the student population was declining every year I was on the board and I simply couldn't logically comprehend why more resources were needed. I could see upgrading technology throughout the division or implementing new programs to replace old ones, but asking for additional personnel never made sense to me. I wanted to know what the budget was for each school, each department, as well as the budget for the school board. Unfortunately, this information was never provided nor was there ever a request made by the majority. Typically, requests were not acted upon unless the majority of the board made it. This practice, I believe, reflected the lack of understanding board members have regarding their fiduciary responsibility and accountability to the taxpayer.

One last mention regarding the process is that it's annual. Key individuals involved complete one year and then immediately begin to prepare for the next year. Since the Virginia General Assembly has a two-year budget cycle, wouldn't this practice be beneficial for local governments as well? The time allocated to preparing and ensuring the budget reaches the approval stage takes months and includes many individuals. Preparing a two-year budget would allow resources more flexibility, as well as the necessary time to adequately gather supporting documentation that should be provided.

Don't Bite the Hand

He who holds the purse strings makes the rules! Though I'm not sure of the origin of this idiom, it's true and was an issue throughout my term. Since the school board didn't have funding authority, they relied on the Board of Supervisors to accept and approve the proposed budget.

Unfortunately, the two boards didn't enjoy a positive working relationship. Since I had previously been appointed to the county planning commission, I had been developing positive relationships since 2007. The majority of the supervisors from when I was appointed to the planning commission were still in office when I was elected to the school board. This was a plus when it came to sharing opinions and discussing recommendations regarding issues that concerned me.

The tension was visible, both verbal and non-verbal, when the schools gave presentations and participated in joint meetings. Comments from both boards were inevitably made that were counter-productive. There was a long history between some members as several individuals on both boards come from families that have been in the county for generations. It's not clear to me why these members didn't seem to get along or try to work together, but I would say for a couple of them it had more to do with agendas, pride, and egos.

I made it a point to be at supervisor meetings when school issues were being presented. I remember during one presentation the school board chair was addressing the need to fund two capital projects. At the end of the presentation a few supervisors expressed their concerns with using existing capital funds and their discomfort with the amount being requested. After responding to a few questions, the chair turned around and moved towards a seat. One supervisor made a comment, which the chair immediately turned around, walked back to the podium, and made an insulting statement regarding the business park the supervisors were moving forward with and the funding appropriated towards that project.

Making derogatory comments that accuse and demean the authority that funds your projects is one example of the types of interactions that burned, not built, bridges.

Spending Priorities

Everyone who seeks public office has an agenda and establishes priorities for what they hope to accomplish. Local officials are no different. However, when school boards establish budget priorities and allocate funds, they should be cultivating an environment focused on providing a quality education, as guaranteed in the Virginia constitution. This commitment should be coupled with ensuring students are afforded the tools, curriculum, and opportunities that enable them to become skilled and functioning adults.

When priorities focus on AstroTurf for the football field, remodeling bathrooms to accommodate social agendas, or facility expansion when student population is decreasing, I consider this an abdication of responsibilities. I'm a firm believer that the focus should be on learning. It's our duty to ensure students are grounded in the basics of reading, writing, and arithmetic. Yes, it's nice to have sports, nice office space, new furniture, and the latest technology, but I consider those to be of lower priority for a division that doesn't generate the necessary revenue.

Budget development will always be contentious. The funding authority wants to give a dollar amount they believe is sufficient, while the education authority believes it's never enough. Reality is local government doesn't have an endless bucket of money and are required by law to maintain a balanced budget. It can only allocate based on the revenue it generates from the taxpayer. That is exactly the reason why taxpayers should participate in the process. If left unchecked, government will continue to raise taxes, fund pet projects, and move forward with determining priorities for you. Is this what you want or expect? I don't!

Data Requests

Receiving what I believed to be sufficient data was the greatest challenge I had when it came to casting my vote. In business, particularly high-performing organizations, data can be overwhelming. There's a tendency to experience *data overload* in an attempt to support decision making. However, receiving too much data was not what I experienced during my term.

Financial Data

I'm not stating that the board didn't receive data. Quite the contrary; data was provided, but it typically reflected a timeframe that was month to month versus an annual period or year-to-year comparisons. For example, each meeting we received financial information, such as accounts payable, payroll, and the monthly financial statement. During my first year the statement would simply be a one-page revenue and expense report. It was high level with six columns starting on the left showing the annual budget for each category, then monthly revenues and expenditures, a year-to-date total, and ending with the balance of funds on the right.

One factor to highlight: The Chief Finance Officer (CFO) was a new hire, which I initially factored into my expectations for a limited period of time. New people always go through a learning curve when they are hired into any organization, regardless of the knowledge and experience they bring. Over the next three years, credit must be given to the CFO for changes that were made due to questions asked in board meetings and the need to align with generally accepted accounting practices (GAAP).

Data that covered multiple years was a request I made during numerous board meetings, which were made with the intent for all members to see the division's monthly finances from year to year. This eventually led to posting previous years' monthly statements. This improvement provided a comparison from the perspective that we could reflect on what the month of March 2018 reported and contrast it to March 2017. During my last year there were five years' worth of financial statements posted for the reported month, which allowed us to identify or recognize any anomalies with revenues and expenditures. I appreciated this advancement with the financials.

In addition, a column was added to the right showing the percent of budget remaining. This information was helpful in that we could see the monthly percentage comparison of what revenues and expenditures were from year to year. For example, if expenditures by the end of March 2018 were 76% and 83% for March 2019, the board would be alerted to inquire as to the cause for a 7% difference. Was there an error or a large expenditure? Is this reflective of an ongoing need? Does the cause need to be factored into the next budget cycle? Being able to identify notable fluctuations of revenues and expenditures gave direction regarding focus and the reason. If adjustments needed to be made, it provided documentation and rationale with future planning efforts.

The reporting of financial data did not meet my expectations based on my business experience, but I give credit to the CFO for improvements made during my term.

Test Scores

One category routinely reported was data related to the annual testing known as Standards of Learning (SOL). Every year test results were provided, as this was the foremost measure of success for the division. The primary reason for this was it's a mandatory requirement from the state. Test scores were required to be reported by a specific date following the end of the academic year. Also, it gave the board a snapshot of the health and level of student learning.

Despite challenges, the majority of the schools reflected passing numbers. The scores were sliced and diced to reflect subject, gender, race, English learner, disabled student, and other demographic categories. Again, multiple years' worth of data were not provided to determine a trend. The usual presentation compared current year to previous year, which didn't adequately indicate whether there was any pattern and what should be analyzed. It was presumed and stated on more than one occasion by both the chair and administration that members were provided what was needed and didn't need details. However, I believe the board's fiduciary responsibility overrides administration decisions. Necessary information should be provided in order to make informed decisions that support appropriate and necessary steps to take.

One issue that skewed this data was the authorized retesting that occurred. If students didn't get a passing score, they were allowed to retest. As a reminder, test results are one factor that determines funding. If students don't do well, their failure has the potential to negatively impact the amount and type of funds provided. On the other hand, when students don't do well, their failure becomes an excuse for the administration to say they don't receive enough funds to meet student needs. As usual, it boils down to funding.

I'm not a fan of SOLs, because they allow teachers and administrators to become complacent and lazy. In one discussion I had with a teacher, I was told, "You just don't understand." Because of the requirement to meet SOL criteria, there was limited time to allow for deviation and creativity. My response was something like, "Surely there must be some type of engaging project students will enjoy doing that can also cover the criteria?" The teacher stated there was that possibility, so I suggested they might want to give it a try. However, the issue seemed to be more about changing existing lesson plans, which would require extra time and effort. I walked away from that conversation thinking it's sad the focus wasn't centered on introducing activities that engaged and enhanced student learning.

The Value of Data

There were too many meetings to count where Ms. Blue or I would ask questions regarding various graphics and data that were presented. Based on our business backgrounds and similar mindset on this topic, we knew the value sufficient data provided in substantiating and supporting decision-making. People in leadership positions understand that data provides value. It reveals trends, shows where adjustments need to be made, whether a program is successful or not, and determines where strengths and weaknesses remain. These elements are important for ensuring whether or not an organization is merely surviving, improving, or growing.

The majority of the board members were reluctant to share too much data for a variety of reasons, the number one being, I believe, is how it would look or be interpreted by the public. When the numbers didn't shine a positive light on the division, the probability was higher that information would be suppressed. This is the wrong mindset to have, particularly since public schools are funded via taxation. When constituents are informed, whether positively or negatively, they are equipped to make decisions. They can choose to support or reject a proposed project or program. And trust me, the majority of people in the public domain know when they are being lied to or scammed.

Later in my term I received a call from a parent who homeschooled her children. She called because of written correspondence they'd received from the Office of the Assistant Superintendent. Since I was not aware of the letter, I informed the parent I'd have to get back with them. I was always infuriated when we were not notified about specific efforts or outreaches made to the public. When constituents called with questions, we couldn't answer them and therefore we appeared ignorant. Unfortunately, this happened on more than one occasion. It's important for staff to keep board members apprised of outreach efforts so we can intelligently address the issues and make sure correct information is shared. Too often misinformation was shared, which only caused more work in order to correct the resulting errors.

This particular outreach was an effort by the division to survey homeschool parents and ask if they would enroll their children in public school if offered an online program. I sent an email inquiring about the letter and was told it was an attempt to bring homeschool students back into the system. It clearly was an effort to increase student population, which is the primary factor related to annual appropriations. This attempt by the division is an example of the arrogance and ignorance of public school administrators and their lack of understanding as to why parents choose to homeschool.

Building trust between the system and the public is critical to sustaining a growing student population. This lack of trust was an issue where I served and the result was parents opted for alternatives, such as homeschooling. Since it wasn't typical for the administration to provide compiled data, I began tracking the number of homeschool students during my first year. In the four years I served, the number of homeschoolers went from 350 to a high of 621. This didn't include the 168 children who filed under Religious Exemption status, according to the last numbers provided. This data clearly reflected two trends: the public student population was decreasing and the homeschool population was increasing.

We didn't have data that showed students moving to private school, but based on my contacts, I'm aware that one of the two private schools in the county was realizing an increase in student population. However, their numbers reflected children from the two surrounding school divisions.

Health of an Organization

Using data in a manner that supports the health of an organization is paramount. During one meeting the subject of *governance* was brought up by the chair and we were provided a governing document used in another division. Ms. Blue and I were in agreement that this was a positive, which could possibly help alleviate some of the contention between board members. I, for one, was in favor of establishing some expectations for how the board should operate in a more cohesive manner. We needed to operate more like a team.

Ms. Blue and I volunteered to be on the governance committee to revise the document and present it to the board for discussion at a future meeting. The two of us created a plan, which included developing questions, conducting interviews with each board member to get their input, and drafting a governance document germane to our division. Based on the interviews, we presented the results at a subsequent meeting.

One idea that came from doing this exercise was to have an off-site to discuss governance and develop a board-driven strategic plan. The members agreed to schedule a facilitated strategy session. It was planned, held, and went no further.

Also, the draft governance document was sent, on at least two separate occasions, to all board members for input and no feedback was ever provided. However, on a couple of occasions, the chair chastised Ms. Blue and me, in public meetings, for not moving forward on governance and then disbanded the governance committee. This clearly reflected no will by the majority to have a governing document with which to define a process and be held accountable.

The willingness and commitment of any organization is manifested in the efforts that focus on organizational health. Building teams is difficult. Simply meeting once a month and voting on routine, sometimes non-relevant, issues isn't a sign of a competent, fully functioning, healthy organization. It takes all parties involved in the decision making to discuss, negotiate, express empathy for, and attempt to understand both sides of any issue. A team will never agree on everything, but decisions need to be made and should be made based on full disclosure.

There are many reasons for an organization to gather and use data. The most relevant is to know where the organization stands in relation to meeting identified goals and objectives. Data also helps provide guidance to determine if a reach is too far or going the distance is attainable. However, when survivability isn't a concern, these viewpoints take on less urgency. When complacency invades and becomes the norm, it's terminal in the private sector. In the public sector, at worst, it causes a shift of personnel and resources. We should expect better from our tax dollars and for our future, because children are our future!

Accountability and Responsibility

The issue of accountability and responsibility really grates on me, particularly since the taxpayer provides the funds that enable communities to have a public education system. Without taxation, in all probability we would be experiencing a different system. On the other hand, having a system that doesn't rely solely on taxation may be a positive, not a negative. But, I digress!

Accountable Persons
The system has a wide range of individuals and groups that are expected to be accountable, but the reality is, few are held accountable. The system consists of legislators, school boards, administrators, principals, and teachers. To a large extent, the system has removed responsibility out of the hands of parents, so for this discussion I'll refrain from speaking specifically about parents and students. For the record, I believe parents should be held accountable and shoulder the responsibility, but the current system doesn't and

in some cases doesn't want them engaged. There are many reasons why the system excuses parents and students, but that's for the next book.

The majority of state constitutions stipulate that a quality education is guaranteed to its citizenry. Legislators are responsible for writing and passing bills that support, not hinder, the delivery of this quality education. In addition, legislation (federal and state) has a tendency to provide mandates without attaching any level of funding. When legislators begin to propose bills making bathrooms gender neutral, stipulating buses must be painted yellow, or requiring that playgrounds only have equipment made of plastic material, I wonder what these issues have to do with providing a quality education. What is the academic value to the student? Isn't the primary intent of education to ensure children learn the basics of reading, writing, and arithmetic? There certainly is a significant amount of pressure inflicted by the system to ensure test scores for these three subjects are as high as possible. Therefore, I'm not convinced legislation that promotes a bias political culture and social agendas ensures a child learns what is needed to be successful in life.

What about school boards? They are appointed or elected into positions of leadership. Their goals should incorporate reasonable, realistic, and affordable programs. They should make sure public funds are expended wisely and propose capital projects that are necessary for student learning and are managed well.

The persons who undertake the day-to-day accountability are administrators, principals, and teachers. These individuals are the boots on the ground. They see in real time what is or isn't working and have the responsibility to manage the classrooms in an orderly, safe, and responsible manner.

Local School Boards

Ultimately, I believe boards must be held accountable for what occurs within the division. They are the leadership that create and convey the vision or at least should be. They are responsible for developing a strategy that supports the learning environment. It's this group of officials who lead with intention to move the division in an identified direction in order to achieve defined goals and objectives.

How does a school board member, who has no K-12 education experience, participate in leading a division? Personally, I believe it's good to have non-educators on school boards. They bring a different perspective to the discussion. They are able to shed light on issues based on the experience they have acquired. They don't perpetuate the status quo by being a part of the system for ten, twenty, or thirty years. It's always good to gain a different understanding through incorporating diversity, interjecting creativity, and shaking up the norm.

As for me, I researched various topics regarding education. I involved myself in conversations that enabled me to be cognizant of pressing issues parents were concerned about, what administrators perceived as priorities, the expected level of community involvement, funding constraints, and more. Also, speaking with a range of interested parties and scanning social media gave me great insight. But, from an accountability and responsibility perspective, attending formal training was the catalyst to understanding the roles and responsibilities of serving on the board.

For whatever reason, it's common for members to attend the monthly meetings and simply rely on hearing from the public on various issues. For me, this doesn't develop effective members. We all need a general awareness of policies, players, and what the expectations are before we can adequately and rationally make decisions.

It's important to acknowledge one's strengths and weaknesses. I believe my lack of knowledge and understanding of the inner workings of the environment I was elected to serve was a weakness. However, I did have awareness based on my experience teaching in higher education and had been involved in politics at the local level for several years. In the end I knew what I stood for, relied on my business experience and instincts to guide me, and turned my weakness into a strength.

School Board Associations

All states have a school board association that provides training, conferences, webinars, policy development, legal support, and other services. In Virginia, it's the Virginia School Board Association (VSBA). This is where I and other members participated in formal training sessions. Some of the courses I took included New Member Orientation, Superintendent Evaluation, Hot Topic Sessions (which varied each year), and the Capital Conference. Members who became Chair or Vice-Chair were offered a course to help them navigate the related role and responsibilities for those positions.

All members are accountable to their constituents and have responsibilities as public officials. Taking courses designed to prepare members with the necessary tools to be effective gives an element of assurance to the public that decisions are made based on understanding. It's also important to have relevant and supporting information.

Not all members of the board I served on participated in formal training, which I found rather unfortunate and to some degree negligent. No one who is elected to a board is automatically endowed with the knowledge and experience needed to make informed decisions. For example, public boards are required to conduct meetings in accordance with Robert's Rules of Order, a parliamentary structure to conduct formal, organized meetings. These rules help ensure all members are given the opportunity and courtesy to speak and be heard on the given issues, votes are based on motions and seconded, meetings are recorded in the form of minutes and made public, and transparency is exhibited.

An important point to make is that school board associations are lobbing organizations. They advocate for specific proposed legislation and ensure all school boards are informed on the legislation they believe should be passed. They actively encourage members to call legislators. There's nothing wrong with this as long as they follow the laws related to their activities. However, when a board member doesn't agree with the espoused VSBA position, don't be surprised when your colleagues make attempts to shame you, in public.

One last point, don't be surprised when a member reaches out to the state association seeking information or requests a legal read on an issue and the superintendent or chair brings up the issue in a public meeting. Or, the superintendent or chair wants to meet with the member to discuss the issue, which wasn't an issue discussed prior to contacting the association. Confidentiality is not necessarily a priority when it appears a member has stepped outside the perceived boundaries.

Issues before a Board

Most meetings consisted of routine agenda items such as voting to approve financials, personnel actions, student fieldtrips and fund-raising events, and meeting minutes. There were times when unique actions were introduced, such as presenting a new procurement manual, which was not a monthly or annual action. Agenda items like this were out of the ordinary and not necessarily a concern with all members. But, it is an important issue because it documents how the division handles buying goods and services on two fronts: procurement policy and funding.

Let's consider teacher pay. All members were interested in this issue and each one had their own perspective on the matter. The standard pay scale reflects steps and years, similar to the federal general schedules or GS pay scale. Salaries are the largest annual expenditure most boards vote on. States are realizing a need to become creative on this subject due to ballooning budgets, in part due to health insurance and retirement pension plans. An abundance of articles espouses that teacher pay is the primary concern when discussing retention. Based on many conversations I've had with teachers, I don't agree. It may be an issue, but in today's environment there are other pressing matters such as safety, administrative support, and simply being appreciated.

School bus issues are another example. There are times when roads are being resurfaced or a bridge was washed out due to severe weather. Routes must be adjusted, which causes a lot of angst for families, as well as the drivers. Also, what happens on buses can be very disturbing. Since the driver must focus on driving, they're not able to adequately monitor the children. Some get into fights, sell drugs, bully younger children, or engage in sexual harassment. Today, most buses have cameras. When an incident is reported, it's common practice to review the recording to help determine what occurred, who was involved, and how the incident should be adjudicated.

Something else I've noticed is there seems to be typical characteristics relatable to members. Boards address and take positions on a range of issues, but I believe votes are not necessarily based on understanding, levels of concern differ, and the majority will often defer to the chair when an issue is believed to be controversial. As you might have guessed, I wasn't a typical public school board member.

Issues in Schools

Teachers have shared with me they went into the profession because they believed it's a calling. They loved being a positive influence and helping children realize they were capable of learning, for example, math or a foreign language. More recently, some have shared concerns related to class size, workload, and especially, student behavior

Unfortunately, today's environment tolerates behaviors I thought would never be permissible on school property or in the classroom. School board members from around the state with whom I've spoken have shared incidents, such as cursing out teachers or assaulting staff and other students, which go unpunished. They report cases where weapons are brought to school or found in a vehicle. However, whether the weapon is a gun, knife, or brass knuckles and if it's reported, then some degree of punishment is doled out.

Not just teachers, but administrators have shared challenges they've encountered regarding the amount of time spent dealing with discipline. An elementary principal relayed an experience involving a disruptive child who regularly kicked, bit, and lashed out with no regard to authority. The parents were no help in correcting the inappropriate behavior. Sadly, this is not a one-off experience with more and more of these situations occurring. Disruptive behavior has become too commonplace. And this is occurring in elementary school!

What can teachers and administrators do? Unfortunately, they have limited options given the current system. They can call the parents, but this is becoming more of a problem, not a solution, because too many parents aren't engaged or interested in their child's education. A child can be sent back to the classroom, but this generally exacerbates the situation and causes further disruption. Or, the child can sit in the office for a period of time to *cool down*, as expulsion or suspension isn't typically an option for dealing with disruptive behavior in the elementary school years.

Adults in the Room

Most people would typically state that accountability and responsibility reside with the teacher, the one in control of the classroom. However, this is not necessarily the case. For teachers to be held accountable and responsible, they have to understand the expectations, know their boundaries with students, and have support from the administration. The rules are not consistently conveyed, let alone shared on a regular basis.

Teachers, like all of us, get complacent over time. We become familiar with our routine, the students, and the environment. However, some teachers take liberties and get involved to a degree where it becomes inappropriate behavior. Whether it's with other teachers or with students, professional norms must be consistently communicated. Consequences must be administered in order to minimize or prevent inappropriate actions from becoming a norm.

Too many cross the line by socializing off school property, participating in activities that display poor judgment, speaking down to students, or going so far as to engage in sexual activity. Teachers who host parties at their residences for minor students and condone alcohol and drug use are not the type of role model I would expect. What about teachers who call students stupid, in front of the class, for being unable to answer a question? What reaction would you, as a parent, have when your child informs you their teacher consistently falls asleep in the classroom? These actions are examples of building walls that hinder learning. Again, this is unacceptable behavior from the adult.

What about reporting these types of behavior? There are several reasons why incidents are not reported and most revolve around fear: the fear of losing their job, retaliation, or bad press the division would receive if the public were informed. I believe these are simply excuses, but I do understand the mindset. No one wants to lose their livelihood because they tried to do what they believed was right. On the other hand, the harm done to children has the potential to last a lifetime. So, people must begin to speak up and speak out!

Not all teachers act in this manner, but any teacher that demonstrates this type of behavior and deems these actions as acceptable would be unwelcome as a teacher in any division I serve.

There are many individuals involved in the education system. But, until the adults, including parents, begin to exert their authority, understand who is accountable, and recognize their responsibility, inappropriate behavior will continue without appropriate consequences.

The Customer

If you read any literature or articles about education, you'll typically be told *children* are the customer and decisions are made based on what's in their best interest. The majority of state constitutions allude to or clearly state the purpose is to provide a *quality education for all*. The truth is, like any business, there's a range of customers based on one's definition. Situations and circumstances typically decide who is a customer, whether they are internal or external, and the priority they are given.

Definition of Customer

I often say *words have meaning* and for that reason we must be intentional with the words we choose. We must equally know the meaning of and understand the words being used in order to convey a concept, idea, or plan.

Merriam-Webster online provides the following definition for customer: 1) *one that purchases a commodity or service*; or 2) *an individual usually having some specified distinctive trait*. Both definitions can be applicable within the education system. There are many who purchase a commodity or service and this could include families, teachers, administrators, and associations. The second definition can be related to those mentioned, but I'd expand the collective group to include communities, churches, other government bodies, and non-profits. The above are not meant to be all-inclusive, but to give a general understanding of the range of individuals and groups that should be considered.

As identified, customer encompasses a broad base and can be difficult to identify, support, manage, and, above all, keep satisfied. In addition, they are generally referred to as internal and external. Hence, it's important to understand what product or service an institution is providing. In general, there's a lesson to be learned from the private sector. The more narrow the focus, the higher the probability of providing a quality product or service. The broader the focus, the more difficult it is to provide quality and keep customers satisfied.

For example, lets consider establishments where we choose to eat. When I select a restaurant that has a menu with three to five pages of offerings, I have a difficult time choosing what I want to order. When I go to a coffee shop or café where the menu is limited, it's less of a challenge to decide between a croissant and a bagel. For one thing, I like croissants more. To me they are less chewy, lighter, and easier to eat. Not that I don't like bagels, but we all choose based on our preferences, likes and dislikes, and our choice of selections. This is analogous to education given the choices offered and customers the system assists.

Internal Customer

This category points to the many entities that work within the system. Within every school there are students, teachers, at least one principal, support staff such as custodian and cafeteria workers, and office administrators. This can equate to thirty to forty persons or up to hundreds of persons. How does the system deal with these customers and keep them satisfied? They typically don't.

There will always be at least one or two persons who are disgruntled about something at sometime. Based on the situation and circumstances, issues are handled in a different manner the majority of the time, because the system can't eliminate the human factor. It's ever-present and what's good for one isn't necessarily good for the other. This is why it's important to identify the expectations and be consistent in application so a toxic culture can be minimized. I've found that when people know what is expected of them, they either rise to the occasion or choose to move on.

School divisions do have policies and regulations that are available for the public to view. My experience brought awareness that the state school board association worked with a legal firm who wrote and supported the policy, which stemmed from the legislation passed and signed into law. Policy would then be provided to the school divisions throughout the state and made available to the public. It's good to have policy and any subsequent regulations, but when these legal pronouncements are not adhered to or applied consistently, problems arise and a legal remedy is one tool used to make adjustments.

One of the inconsistencies I recognized early on was the lack of hiring practices and procedures utilized. For example, not all positions were advertised. Yes, there was an ongoing blurb on the division website about the need to hire teachers, but when it came to certain positions, it was more of *who you know* as to whether the public even knew a position was available. As a business professional and a professor who taught human resources courses, this was disturbing to me.

When it came to hiring for business positions such as the Director of Technology or Human Resources or Operations, I let it be known that I vehemently opposed hiring teachers or administrators for these positions. It's not that teaches can't learn, but it's more a matter of those who grow up in the system perpetuate the status quo. There is some legitimacy to hiring from within, but it's more legitimate to hire for skills, experience, and knowledge when seeking to hire for business positions.

Another inconsistency was how teachers who came before the board were treated. The reality is each circumstance was different because each scenario represented one person who had done something someone determined to be offensive. The proposed remedy was intended to be applicable to the situation. However, it was clear which teachers the superintendent and certain board members favored. Unfortunately, other teachers had little recourse and I believe fear of retaliation was always an underlying factor.

One may wonder how consistency could be applied to separate and distinct circumstances. It's because there is policy on how to handle discipline, whether it's related to staff or students. Though policy may have gray areas, remedies are identified in the various policies and should be applied equally, based on the provided guidance.

External Customer

There's an array of entities that provide support, but are external to the system. They range from contractors to churches to non-profits to other state and federal government agencies. As previously mentioned, the county Board of Supervisors is the funding source for the school division and the relationships between the two boards should be a priority.

Churches and non-profits serve many needs for various children and their families. They gather forces to provide food, school supplies, clothing, private funding, and moral support, as well as other needs that have been identified within the division. An example I experienced involved a non-profit along with several concerned citizens who came before the board to petition a change in policy regarding school lunches. The policy applied one remedy for elementary students with overdue lunch balances while a different remedy was afforded to middle and high school students. This distinction led to a couple of what I would refer to as contentious meetings. Passionate adults who spoke during the public comment period were proposing solutions and trying to ensure that children would be provided a lunch, even if they didn't pay for it.

My position on this subject was that parents are responsible for ensuring their children are fed. They could pack a lunch, pay for a school lunch, or apply for the free and reduced lunch program. In one meeting during public comment a former employee spoke and stated that there's a stigma associated with families who apply for low-income lunch programs. I viewed this as an excuse. Because parents are either proud or uninformed about free and reduced lunch programs, the argument is that it's important for the schools to forgive the debt or ensure the community provides a solution? I'm not in agreement on this one.

I do agree it's a shame that some children have irresponsible parents and go hungry, but the primary issue being discussed revolved around the inconsistency within the policy. It provided one remedy at the lower grade levels and another at the upper grade levels. However, the reality was all children were being fed. While the food wasn't always the preferred choice, they all were given a meal.

As a policy geek, I agreed that consistency for all the children is the solution, regardless of the grade. After a couple of months of public comments along with various related Facebook posts and news articles, the board approved the recommended changes, which brought the two policies in alignment across the grade levels. In addition, the non-profit reported they raised enough money to help pay for many of the overdue balances, which would be applied to student accounts based on the administration's recommendation.

Another example of external customers involved a family who chose to homeschool. In Virginia, parents who plan to homeschool their children are required to submit notification via a notice of intent. This population continued to increase in numbers, which was a dilemma, because student population is one of the major determining factors related to funding. When there is a decrease in the number of students attending public school, the amount of public dollars provided to the division theoretically experiences a decrease as well. However, it's perplexing to me as to why the annual budget requests continued to increase every year.

This led to another policy dispute in 2018, when the case *Sosebee et al. v. Franklin County School Board* ended up in court. The administration decided to modify the homeschool policy so that it imposed additional requirements on homeschoolers that exceeded what the state code specified. The proposed change was presented to the board for a vote. Having been informed by a homeschool constituent, I was alerted to the proposed change. Let me state that at that time it was the typical practice to post a listing of new or amended policy within a few days to a week before the board was expected to vote. During my term the board never met to discuss policy prior to a meeting. The expectation was that administration or VSBA recommendations would be acceptable, which was typically the case for the majority.

However, this family disagreed with the policy change and reached out to the Home School Legal Defense Association (HSLDA) seeking assistance. To make a long story short, the case was heard before the district court in Rocky Mount, VA. Despite my expectation of an unfavorable ruling for the family, I chose to attend the hearing in order to hear for myself what was said and hear the judge's decision, which was for the division. The family appealed to the VA Supreme Court, which in June 2020 overturned the lower court. As reported by Justia U.S. Law in the summary, the ruling in part stated:

"The Supreme Court reversed, holding that the Board did not have authority to adopt the policy pursuant to section 22.1-78 because that statute only allows school boards to adopt regulations for the supervision of public schools, not home instruction."

In addition the annotation states the Primary Holding as:

"The Supreme Court reversed the circuit court's judgment denying a request for declaratory and injunctive relief to bar enforcement of the Franklin County School Board's policy requiring parents to provide a birth certificate and proof of residence in the county for any child who is homeschooled, holding that the policy is contrary to the Homeschool Statute."

In my humble opinion, this case was more about the school district's effort to get homeschooled children back into public school in order to deal with the declining funds and impact on the student population. Not to mention that this led to the unnecessary expenditure of taxpayer dollars. Parents choose to homeschool because they are concerned about the education their children receive.

One last example I'd like to share deals with an organization that wanted to provide information to public school employees. Most of you have heard of and participated in a PTA or PTO. Also, there are education associations like the National Education Association (NEA) and American Federal of Teachers (AFT), which are unions. Each state has its own micro version of the NEA, which function as unions and follow similar agendas. However, Virginia is a right-to-work state and employees can't be forced, but have the choice on whether or not to become a member of the state-affiliated association. The above organizations are given access to schools, distribute information, and meet on school property.

This case involved a new education non-profit created by local parents. They thought some issues weren't being addressed, wanted solutions, and didn't convey the same message as the union sanctioned education associations. When the organization went public and requested access to school property to hold meetings and share information, they were denied. The situation escalated to a point where certain school board members requested a modification to policy. The change would ensure only organizations created by employees or retirees of the division could have access to school facilities and distribute information to employees.

A board member in the division where this was occurring contacted me and I shared that I disagree with the policy change. Why shouldn't parents organize and meet on school property to share their concerns? Why not allow them to post information flyers on school bulletin boards? Shouldn't we all be open to listening to a point-counterpoint discussion? From my perspective this is a form of discrimination. Or could it be censorship? Either way, school property is public space and paid for by the taxpayers.

These are examples of where policy should be applied consistently, not overstepping one's authority, and remembering who the customer is. If we expect repeat business, then customer service is crucial. There's a reason it's called public education: because it's there to provide learning opportunities to *the public*. ALL public institutions exist for one reason: to serve *We the People*.

The Ultimate Customer

With such an array of individuals and groups identified as customers, the bottom line is the taxpayer is the ultimate customer. I do agree students should be a focus, because they will grow up to become the individuals that feed the beast. They will become our future taxpayers. Without taxation, there would be no public education system, as we know it.

Doing What's Right

How do you determine what's right? Is what's right for one, right for another? These are good questions that many would claim difficult to answer. On the other hand, I believe they can be rather simple to address.

My Belief
First, I believe we all know instinctively when we are doing something wrong. We have this little voice in our head that lets us know. Some believe this is the voice of God speaking to them. Others refer to it as their conscience. Whatever you believe, the majority of individuals are able to differentiate between appropriate and inappropriate behavior.

When a child hits another child, they know it's inappropriate behavior, particularly once they are told. When someone drives fifty miles an hour in a thirty-mile-an-hour speed zone, they know they are breaking the law. When a student turns in an assignment they copied from another student and hope they don't get caught, that's a clear sign they know they should've taken the time to do their own work. I have faith that most people would agree.

Second, any decision a person or group makes will be right for one and wrong for another. This is the nature of life, because we are individuals, view issues differently, and bring our own set of beliefs to the discussion. For this reason I would like to remind people we're a nation of laws. Persons in authority communicate rules to people and expect compliance.

As a school board member and person who worked for public and private organizations, I've dealt with laws, policy, regulations, and processes over many decades. These fundamentals provide a structure of known standards meant to benefit our lives. They are instructional in nature and meant to be disclosed to the community at large. Governing bodies have the responsibility to ensure they are followed and applied equitably. However, problems arise when an individual or group decides to deviate when applying the established set of standards to one situation, but not to another. I'll refer to this as bias, which causes conflict and promotes a toxic work culture and society.

Sage Advice

When I was running for the school board, I continually sought advice. I remember attending a book signing in 2015 in Tysons Corner, VA where

I happened to have an opportunity to briefly speak with Mark Levin and his wife. Knowing that he was a lawyer who had been involved for many years in the political arena, I asked what advice he'd give me should I win the election. His sage advice was to vote my conscience, because my record is how I would be judged. At that point I began to question myself. Would I be capable of doing what was right and standing on my foundation? Or would I be easily swayed and go against what I stood for? His words resonated with me and I've thought about that brief, yet impactful, conversation many times over the years. I have come to the conclusion that Mark and I have something in common; we each have a belief system that guides our actions and gives definition for what we believe to be right.

Another point I want to share is there's a lot of talk about doing what's fair. Well, I don't believe life if fair, nor do I believe we can expect fairness to be applied to all. I go back to the reality that we are all individuals and what's perceived to be fair to one isn't necessarily fair to another.

Nonetheless, I do believe in equality. This is one reason I'm such a firm believer in words have meaning and the words we use need to be intentional. When it comes to applying the law and making a decision on what consequences should be applied, it's reasonable to expect equality. It's not reasonable to expect fairness.

If it were about fairness, then what definition would be used? Fairness, like beauty, is in the eye of the beholder. Equality, on the other hand, means applying the law in the same manner to all. Everyone gets an apple or no one gets an apple. Unfortunately, we don't consistently receive equal application under the law, as many laws have inequality written into them and this is one of the factors relating to our societal woes. Also, equality (stated and implied) is rooted in our Declaration of Independence and U.S. Constitution; not fairness.

Character Matters

Too many people, particularly in politics, don't have what I'll refer to as moral character. People will do and say what they want without concerning themselves or acknowledging the impact their decisions will have on others. Also, integrity is lacking in today's world. We see this all around us. People are randomly killing others, selling illegal drugs, entering the United States without permission, and deliberately destroying property and people's lives. Countless individuals are focused on gaining or retaining their perceived power and control. Too many people make decisions based on the calculated financial gain they'll receive. Others make decisions for the sheer purpose of imposing their will onto others through fear and intimidation. Understanding how and why decisions are made will give an indication of one's character.

I believe there are many examples where leaders in today's society demonstrate poor character and judgment, and aren't held accountable. Look no further than what the media chooses to report and how they convey news. Watching the nightly news is no longer a way to stay informed. This 24/7 news cycle that's been created is too much, too negative, and doesn't reflect the reality of what's going on in the heartland of this great republic we are privileged to live in.

Look at the poll numbers for our Congressional members in Washington, D.C. As of this writing, the numbers range from 17% to 31% with an average of 25%, depending on the poll one looks at. This seems to indicate people hold little trust in congress' ability or desire to do what's best for the people of our republic. When a budget can't get passed, which is their job, this reflects a lack of performance or unwillingness and edges towards what I believe to be criminal. You and I are expected to live within our means, but congress can legally steal from those who work hard to provide for their families. Congress calls this taxation; I'd call it extortion!

What about the innocent children and adults getting killed in major metropolitan cities every week. Where's the outrage at this death rate? Is it simply because they live in urban neighborhoods?

Is the leadership doing what's right in these situations? I think not!

When a teacher is caught buying alcohol for minor students or a superintendent authorizes a known, convicted sex offender to attend a function at a school his children attend, is this doing what's right? I think not and believe persons in authority who make such egregious decisions should face consequences. Unfortunately, in far too many cases, minimal to no corrective action is taken, unless the public is made aware and speaks out. When situations become public, the typical result will be a reactionary pronouncement rather than ensuring the right thing was done from the beginning.

My response when dealing with personnel cases was always to question what kind of an example we would be setting if we voted to do nothing. What message would we be sending to those who try to do what's right? Over time it appeared to me that doing what's right wasn't valued. For senior administrators, retaining or advancing their position within the system seems to be the objective. Board members appeared to take actions that would ensure winning the next election and helping to maintain the status quo. Like me, naive board members who think they can make positive change would vote their conscience and then choose to leave the system because poor decisions win out. How does any of the above help improve the system?

Unfortunately, taking positive, corrective action becomes almost impossible, because too many others are conforming to the status quo as well as using poor judgment. In the end, the character each board member depicts is based on how they vote, the courage they show, and conviction they demonstrate based on believing they're doing what's right. In the end, I believe I did vote my conscience and made decisions based on what I believe was right.

Final Thoughts

This book is not meant to tell anyone how to act as an elected public school board member or what should be done. It's merely a compilation of some of my experiences and lessons I learned while campaigning, winning an election, and then serving in the position.

Serving one's community is an honor and a privilege. I would highly recommend anyone who believes they can make a difference to give it a go. There is no greater endeavor than to serve others. However, if you choose to serve in a public position, be aware of the environment you will be entering. There are personalities with agendas that aren't necessarily focused on doing what's right and issues can become very political. Enter the arena with courage, conviction, and a willingness to stand strong.

As previously mentioned, accountability and responsibility are central to a healthy organization along with ensuring business is conducted in a manner that is as transparent as possible. Yes, you are part of a team; you are only one vote; but you are also a voice for those who believe they have no voice. Demand excellence, because if you don't, no one else will!

There are three guarantees I can pretty much promise you when dealing with any public body:
1) it's part of a bureaucracy,
2) there are people who don't want change, and
3) communication needs improvement.

Every level of government has bureaucracy. I've worked in several and each one demands patience. There are many layers, both horizontal and vertical. Navigating the maze is challenging and requires you to understand how each layer works or doesn't work together in order to understand where to focus the necessary energy and attention that will support and make improvements.

Regarding the second guarantee, many people don't want to be challenged or have anyone propose and promote change. As a general rule, it's natural for people to be resistant. I can't tell you how many times over my career in federal government I heard the phrase, "It's how we've always done it." This is my number one pet peeve in the workplace. My blood still boils when I hear it. Government organizations have developed a culture with a mindset that drives the status quo. Given this type of thinking and attitude, it's no wonder the education system is decreasing in quality and value to the citizens of our great republic.

The last guarantee centers on poor or non-effective communication. When adults don't encounter or believe they are engaged in helpful communication, it should be expected that concerns and problems would arise. When parents aren't listened to, or are simply ignored, they become numb to working with teachers and administrators. Constituents begin to question whether budgets are realistic and the actions being taken are supporting positive adjustments. In addition, too many students constantly get away with inappropriate behavior in the school setting as expectations are continually lowered and endlessly shifting.

Communication is the key component that relays confidence and builds trust. People are likely to accept more rather than less communication, because less makes people question. It makes parents wonder if they should seek an alternative to traditional public school when they believe they aren't getting answers. All of us become products of our environment and spending seven or more hours, five days a week, in any environment reaps results: *positive and negative*.

Though running for a seat on a local public school board was never on my radar before I made the decision to run, I would not trade my time of serving for anything. This service afforded me the opportunity to learn many aspects of K-12 education in a way no other experience could have provided. It revealed to me good people who truly have a heart for helping children learn as well as the irrational stagnation that's robbing our children of a quality education. While some days were extremely challenging, dealing with issues I couldn't believe we were grappling over; this was a time I will cherish. Representing the public on something so sacred and vital to our communities, country, and world was nothing short of incredible.

Would I run again? Probably not! But, I will never say never as I've had to eat my words too many times in the past. The journey I've taken to date has been a road worth traveling for many reasons. I will say there is no greater calling than to serve the public and work in the field of education. People who genuinely make the choice to help children learn, grow, and develop their God-given talents are exceptional. However, I believe we should expect the system to focus on education and leave the food, shelter, and clothing to parents. Our republic needs a system that produces a well-educated public, not one that creates dependency and mediocrity.

I do want to say a word to parents. From my perspective too many relinquish their role to the system. The system, in some sense, has become the daycare provider for parents who work outside the home. I've also wondered if parents send their children to school in order to enjoy some alone time or simply because they don't want to deal with their child. I believe all of these can be applicable, but to what degree is debatable.

We also seem to be losing the sense of family and what all that involves. We are allowing more and more people to become less accountable and responsible. We are allowing our system to shape minds in a manner and to an extent that we are losing creative thinkers, moral character, and respect for others. I believe too many individuals have lost the ability to make the correlation that hard work equates to achievement and success. Above all, we must get back to developing a work ethic that supports and promotes self-reliance and also honors others by showing dignity and respect.

So, what value is one getting for their tax dollars? What are children learning? Why are children leaving the system? These are questions every parent should ponder and make sure they have answers to. Otherwise, the system will continue with the status quo by doing what it believes is best and perpetuating the reality that parents should remain uninformed consumers.

References

Code of Virginia: Charter School. (2020). *§ 22.1-26. Joint and regional schools; regional public charter schools*. Retrieved from: https://law.lis.virginia.gov/vacode/title22.1/chapter4/section22.1-26/

Code of Virginia: Homeschool. (2020). *§ 22.1-254.1. Declaration of policy; requirements for home instruction of children*. Retrieved from: https://law.lis.virginia.gov/vacode/title22.1/chapter14/section22.1-254.1/

Home School Legal Defense Association (HSLDA). (2020). *Sosebee Decision Confirms It's a "Notice" not a "Request."* Retrieved from: https://hslda.org

Justia U.S. Law. (2020). *Sosebee et al. v. Franklin County School Board*. Retrieved from: https://law.justia.com/cases/virginia/supreme-court/2020/190620.html

Virginia Constitution. (1971). *Article VIII. Education*. Retrieved from: ttps://law.lis.virginia.gov/constitution/article8/

Virginia School Board Association (VSBA). (2020). *Publications and Articles*. Retrieved from: https://www.vsba.org/resources/publications/

About the Author

Dr. Hiltz served in the United States Navy at locations in the United States and England, which acquainted her with supply and budget, and laid the foundation for her career in business.

Her journey led to a career in Federal Acquisition and Procurement, raise three children, graduate with a BA and MBA in Management and an Ed.D in Leadership Studies, teach at undergraduate and graduate levels, run for public office, and become an author and speaker on education.

Her experiences as an elected public school board member, private school board member, appointed member of the Virginia Western Community College Local Advisory Board, and serve on education non-profits has enhanced her passion for being an advocate for education choice. She witnessed and understands the frustrations parents and grandparents have with traditional public school, not knowing if they have options, and questioning where they can turn for help.

She met her husband, Chuck (retired USMC), while serving in San Diego, CA. Their journey continues in Florida.

Other books by Dr. Karen Hiltz

www.ingramcontent.com/pod-product-compliance
Lightning Source LLC
Chambersburg PA
CBHW070944100426
42738CB00010BA/2128